GALVESTON DIET COOKBOOK FOR BEGINNERS

Quick and Delicious Recipes for Hormonal Wellness, Weight Management and Vibrant Health with a 28-Day Meal Plan

SOPHIA DAVIS

© Copyright 2024 Sophia Davis - All rights reserved.

The content contained within this book may not be reproduced, duplicated, or transmitted without direct written permission from the author or the publisher.

Under no circumstances will any blame or legal responsibility be held against the publisher or au-thor for any damages, reparation, or monetary loss due to the information contained within this book, either directly or indirectly.

Legal Notice:

This book is copyright-protected. It is only for personal use. You cannot amend, distribute, sell, use, quote, or paraphrase any part of the content within this book without the consent of the author or publisher.

Disclaimer Notice:

Please note that information contained within this document is for educational and entertainment purposes only. All efforts have been executed to present accurate, up-to-date, reliable, and complete information. No warranties of any kind are declared or implied. Readers acknowledge that the author is not engaged in the rendering of legal, financial, medical, or professional advice. The content within this book has been derived from various sources. Please consult a licensed professional before attempting any techniques outlined in this book.

By reading this document, the reader agrees that under no circumstances is the author responsible for any losses, direct or indirect, that are incurred as a result of the use of the information contained within this document, including, but not limited to, errors, omissions, or inaccuracies.

Table of Content

- Introduction 5
- Breakfast 6
- Tropical Mango Coconut Smoothie 6
- Chocolate Strawberry Smoothie 7
- Mint Chocolate Chip Smoothie 8
- Turmeric Ginger Detox Smoothie 9
- Peanut Butter Banana Smoothie 10
- Quinoa Breakfast Bowl 11
- Greek Yogurt Bowl 12
- Buckwheat Bowl with Chicken and Vegetables 13
- Flaxseed Meal Pancakes with Berries 14
- Oatmeal with Fresh Berries 15
- Spinach Omelette 16
- Oat and Berry Acai Bowl 17
- Avocado and Poached Egg Sandwich 18
- Green Shakshuka 19
- Baked Eggs in Avocado 20
- Coconut Flour Pancakes with Berries 21
- Sweet Potato and Spinach Breakfast Hash 22
- Lunch 23
- Almond Chicken with Broccoli 23
- Stuffed Bell Peppers with Ground Beef and Quinoa 24
- Zoodles with Pesto Sauce and Turkey 25
- Mushroom Cream Soup 26
- Broccoli and Cheese Cream Soup 27
- Vegetable and Nut Stew 28
- Red Lentil and Chicken Stew 29
- Mediterranean Chickpea Salad 30
- Quinoa and Black Bean Salad 31
- Shrimp Avocado Salad 32
- Tuna and White Bean Salad 33
- Avocado and Turkey Wrap 34
- Cheeseburger Lettuce Sliders 35
- Lemon Garlic Turkey Meatballs with Green Beans 36
- Chicken Casserole with Broccoli 37
- Chicken Breast Stuffed Spinach and Cheese with Boiled Vegetables 38
- Dinner 39
- Salmon and Asparagus Foil Packets 39
- Baked Chicken with Brussels Sprouts 40
- Stuffed Zucchini Boats 41
- Greek Chicken Skewers with Cauliflower Rice 42
- Spaghetti Squash with Fish Balls 43
- Baked Cod with Asparagus and Hollandaise Sauce 44

Zucchini Noodles with Pesto and Shrimp 45
Chicken and Vegetable Stir-Fry 46
Grilled Salmon with Avocado Salsa 47
Coconut Shrimp with Mango Salsa 48
Scallop and Warm Spinach Salad 49
Blackened Tofu with Sesame Broccoli Slaw 50
Stuffed Bell Peppers with Quinoa 51
Cauliflower Steak with Tahini Dressing 52
Roasted Beetroot with Herbs 53
Butterfly Salmon Steak with Pesto Sauce 54

Snacks 56
Mushroom Stroganoff with Creamy Garlic Cauliflower Rice 55
Coconut Matcha Energy Balls 56
Kale Chips 57
Smoked Salmon Cucumber Bites 58
Almond Flour Crackers with Guacamole 59
Baba Ganoush 60
Herbed White Bean Dip 61
Mushroom Caviar Dip 62
Deviled Eggs 63
Prosciutto-Wrapped Asparagus 64
Mango Salsa with Jicama Chips 65
Edamame Hummus 66
Stuffed Dates with Almonds and Goat Cheese 67
Eggplant Chips with Tahini Dip 68
Zucchini Fritters 69
Walnut Cocoa Balls 70

Desserts 71
Pumpkin Oatmeal Cookies 71
Zucchini Carrot Muffins 72
Avocado Chocolate Brownies 73
Grilled Pineapple with Coconut Whipped Cream 74
Chocolate Avocado Mousse 75
Chia Seed Pudding with Mango 76
Pumpkin Pie Chia Pudding 77
Coconut Macaroons 78
Coconut Milk Panna Cotta with Raspberry Sauce 79
Blueberry Almond Crumble 80
Galveston Diet Texas Sheet Cake 81
Yogurt Berry Ice Cream 82
Chocolate-Cinnamon Apple Bites 83
Blueberry Peach Cobbler 84
Lemon Ricotta Berry Parfait 85

28-Day Meal Plan 86
Conclusion 88

Introduction

Welcome to a healthier, more vibrant you with the «Galveston Diet Cookbook for Beginners»! This comprehensive guide is your gateway to a transformative lifestyle rooted in scientific research, where harmony with your body's natural rhythms leads to lasting well-being and sustainable weight management. This cookbook is your compass on an exciting journey to health, offering delicious and nutritious recipes that help you achieve your goals without sacrificing the joy of eating.

The Galveston Diet is more than just another diet; it's a holistic lifestyle focused on restoring metabolic health, reducing inflammation, and supporting hormonal balance. Developed by Dr. Mary Claire Haver, this diet blends intermittent fasting ideas with the consumption of anti-inflammatory foods, allowing you to achieve optimal health without restrictive measures and while enjoying every meal.

The Galveston Diet offers key benefits such as sustainable weight loss, improved metabolic health, and enhanced overall well-being. It supports your body by helping to control blood sugar levels, boosting energy, and reducing inflammation.

As you embark on your journey with the Galveston Diet Cookbook for Beginners, it's important to approach this lifestyle change with patience and flexibility. Start by gradually incorporating the principles of the diet into your routine. Focus on the delicious, anti-inflammatory foods that nourish your body and support your overall health. Recall that consistency is essential; little, gradual changes will lead to lasting results. Take advantage of the 28-day meal plan and the diverse recipes provided in this book to keep your meals exciting and aligned with your health goals.

We hope this cookbook becomes your trusted companion in the kitchen, inspiring you to create meals that are as delicious as they are nutritious. Whether you're new to the Galveston Diet or simply looking to refresh your meal rotation, may you find joy in every recipe and success in your journey to a healthier you. Happy cooking, and enjoy your reading!

BREAKFAST

2 serving

0 minutes

5 minutes

Tropical Mango Coconut Smoothie

Ingredients

- 1 cup frozen mango chunks
- 1/2 cup canned coconut milk
- 1 avocado
- 2 scoops of unflavored or vanilla protein powder (about 30g per scoop)
- 2 tbsp unsweetened shredded coconut
- 1 cup unsweetened almond milk
- Ice cubes (optional)

Instructions

1. Gather all the ingredients.

2. In a blender, combine the frozen mango chunks, canned coconut milk, avocado (peeled and pitted), protein powder, unsweetened shredded coconut, and unsweetened almond milk. If desired, add a few ice cubes for extra chilliness.

3. Blend all the ingredients until smooth and creamy. If the consistency is too thick, you can add more almond milk to reach your desired consistency.

4. Pour the smoothie into two glasses and garnish with a sprinkle of shredded coconut on top, if desired.

Nutrition: Cal 362; Fat 24g; Carb 21g; Protein 21g

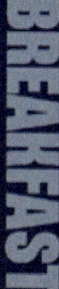

2 serving

0 minutes

5 minutes

BREAKFAST

Chocolate Strawberry Smoothie

Ingredients

- 2 scoops protein powder
- 2 cups chopped fresh kale
- 1 cup sliced fresh strawberries
- 2 tbsp ground flaxseed
- 2 tbsp unsweetened almond butter
- 2 tbsp unsweetened cocoa powder
- 1 cup coconut milk
- 4 tbsp chia seeds
- Ice cubes (optional)

Instructions

1. Gather all the ingredients.

2. In a blender, combine the protein powder, chopped kale, sliced strawberries, ground flaxseed, almond butter, cocoa powder, coconut milk, and chia seeds. Add ice cubes if desired.

3. Blend all the ingredients until smooth and creamy. If the consistency is too thick, you can add more coconut milk to reach your desired consistency.

4. Pour the smoothie into glasses and serve immediately.

Nutrition: Cal 330; Fat 18g; Carb 25g; Protein 23g

BREAKFAST

2 serving

0 minutes

5 minutes

Mint Chocolate Chip Smoothie

Ingredients

- 2 cups spinach
- 1 avocado
- 2 scoops unflavored or chocolate protein powder
- 2 tbsp cocoa nibs or dark chocolate chips
- 1/2 tsp peppermint extract
- 2 cups unsweetened almond milk
- Ice cubes (optional)

Instructions

1. Gather all the ingredients.
2. In a blender, combine the spinach, avocado, protein powder, cocoa nibs or dark chocolate chips, peppermint extract, and unsweetened almond milk. Add ice cubes if desired.
3. Blend all the ingredients until smooth and creamy. If the consistency is too thick, you can add more almond milk to reach your desired consistency.
4. Pour the smoothie into glasses and serve immediately.

Nutrition: Cal 320; Fat 18g; Carb 17g; Protein 25g

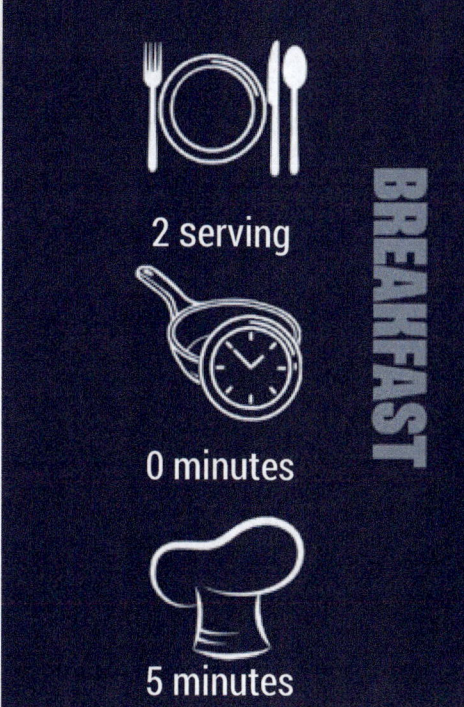

2 serving

0 minutes

5 minutes

BREAKFAST

Turmeric Ginger Detox Smoothie

Ingredients

- 2 cups unsweetened almond milk
- 1 frozen banana, halved
- 1 tsp ground turmeric
- 2 tsp grated ginger
- 2 tbsp chia seeds
- 2 scoops unflavored or vanilla protein powder
- Dash of black pepper (to enhance turmeric absorption)
- Ice cubes (optional)

Instructions

1. Gather all the ingredients.
2. In a blender, combine the unsweetened almond milk, frozen banana halves, ground turmeric, grated ginger, chia seeds, protein powder, and a dash of black pepper. Add ice cubes if desired.
3. Blend all the ingredients until smooth and creamy. If the consistency is too thick, you can add more almond milk to reach your desired consistency.
4. Pour the smoothie into glasses and serve immediately.

Nutrition: Cal 270; Fat 9g; Carb 27g; Protein 22g

BREAKFAST

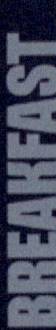

2 serving

0 minutes

5 minutes

Peanut Butter Banana Smoothie

Ingredients

- 1 ripe banana, sliced
- 2 tbsp natural peanut butter
- 2 scoops unflavored or vanilla protein powder
- 2 cups unsweetened almond milk
- Ice cubes (optional)

Instructions

1. Gather all the ingredients.
2. In a blender, combine the sliced ripe banana, natural peanut butter, protein powder, and unsweetened almond milk. Add ice cubes if desired.
3. Blend all the ingredients until smooth and creamy. If the consistency is too thick, you can add more almond milk to reach your desired consistency.
4. Pour the smoothie into glasses and serve immediately.

Nutrition: Cal 310; Fat 13g; Carb 23g; Protein 27g

2 serving

15 minutes

15 minutes

BREAKFAST

Quinoa Breakfast Bowl

Ingredients

- 1 cup cooked quinoa
- 2 tbsp almond butter
- 1 banana, sliced
- Sprinkle of cinnamon
- Drizzle of honey (optional)

Instructions

1. If quinoa is not already cooked, prepare it according to package instructions.
2. Divide the cooked quinoa evenly between two bowls.
3. Top each bowl of quinoa with 1 tbsp of almond butter.
4. Add sliced banana on top of the almond butter.
5. Sprinkle cinnamon over the bowls to taste.
6. Drizzle honey over the bowls if using

Nutrition: Cal 310; Fat 12 g; Carb 45 g; Protein 9g

BREAKFAST

2 serving

0 minutes

15 minutes

Greek Yogurt Bowl

Ingredients

- 1 cup plain Greek yogurt (full-fat, unsweetened)
- 1/4 cup fresh berries (such as blueberries, strawberries, or raspberries)
- 2 tbsp chopped nuts (such as almonds or walnuts)
- 1 tbsp chia seeds
- 1 tsp flax seeds (optional)
- 1 tsp honey or a few drops of stevia (optional for sweetness)
- Fresh mint leaves for garnish (optional)

Instructions

1. Divide the Greek yogurt equally between two bowls.
2. Top each bowl of yogurt with fresh berries, chopped nuts, chia seeds, and flax seeds (if using).
3. Drizzle a small amount of honey or add a few drops of stevia to each bowl if you prefer a sweeter taste.
4. Garnish with fresh mint leaves if desired.

Nutrition: Cal 250; Fat 15g; Carb 15g; Protein 15g

2 serving

15 minutes

10 minutes

BREAKFAST

Buckwheat Bowl with Chicken and Vegetables

Ingredients

For the Bowl:
- 1/2 cup buckwheat groats
- 1 cup water or low-sodium chicken broth (for cooking buckwheat)
- 1 chicken breast, cooked and sliced
- 1 cup cherry tomatoes, halved
- 1 cup cucumber, diced
- 1 cup microgreens (such as arugula, radish, or pea shoots)

For the Sesame Sauce:
- 2 tbsp tahini
- 1 tbsp soy sauce or tamari (for gluten-free)
- 1 tbsp sesame oil
- 1 tbsp rice vinegar
- 1 tsp honey or maple syrup (optional)
- 1 clove garlic, minced
- 1 tsp grated fresh ginger
- 1-2 tbsp water (to thin the sauce, as needed)
- Sesame seeds for garnish (optional)

Instructions

1. Rinse buckwheat groats under cold water.
2. In a medium saucepan, bring 1 cup of water or chicken broth to a boil.
3. Add buckwheat groats, reduce heat to low, cover, and simmer for about 10-12 minutes, or until tender and the liquid is absorbed.
4. Fluff with a fork and let cool slightly.

  Sesame Sauce:
5. In a small bowl, whisk together tahini, soy sauce or tamari, sesame oil, rice vinegar, honey or maple syrup (if using), minced garlic, and grated ginger.
6. Add water a little at a time until you reach your desired sauce consistency. It should be pourable but thick enough to coat the ingredients.

  Assemble the Bowl:
7. Divide the cooked buckwheat evenly between two bowls.
8. Top with sliced chicken breast, cherry tomatoes, diced cucumber, and microgreens.
9. Drizzle with sesame sauce.
10. Sprinkle sesame seeds over the top for added texture and flavor.

Nutrition: Cal   400;   Fat   20g;   Carb   30g;   Protein   25g

BREAKFAST

2 serving

10 minutes

5 minutes

Flaxseed Meal Pancakes with Berries

Ingredients

- 2 eggs
- 4 tbsp flaxseed meal
- 1/2 tsp baking powder
- Splash of unsweetened almond milk (as needed for consistency)
- Coconut oil for cooking
- Handful of mixed berries for topping

Instructions

1. In a mixing bowl, beat the eggs until well combined.
2. Add the flaxseed meal and baking powder to the beaten eggs, and mix until smooth. If the batter is too thick, add a splash of unsweetened almond milk to reach your desired consistency.
3. Heat a non-stick skillet over medium heat and add a small amount of coconut oil to coat the surface.
4. Once the skillet is hot, pour a portion of the batter onto the skillet to form pancakes of your desired size.
5. Cook the pancakes for 2-3 minutes on one side or until bubbles form on the surface.
6. Carefully flip the pancakes and cook for an additional 1-2 minutes on the other side, or until golden brown and cooked through.
7. Repeat the process with the remaining batter, adding more coconut oil to the skillet as needed.
8. Once all the pancakes are cooked, stack them on serving plates. Top each stack of pancakes with a handful of mixed berries.

Nutrition: Cal 220; Fat 16g; Carb 4g; Protein 12g

2 serving

15 minutes

10 minutes

BREAKFAST

Oatmeal with Fresh Berries

Ingredients

For the Oatmeal:
- 1 cup rolled oats
- 2 cups water or unsweetened almond milk (for creamier oatmeal)
- 1/4 tsp salt (optional)
- 1/2 tsp ground cinnamon (optional)

For the Toppings:
- 1/2 cup fresh blueberries
- 1/2 cup fresh strawberries, sliced
- 1/4 cup fresh raspberries
- 1-2 tbsp honey or maple syrup (optional)
- 1 tbsp chia seeds or flaxseeds (optional)

Instructions

1. In a medium saucepan, bring 2 cups of water or almond milk to a boil.
2. Add the rolled oats and a pinch of salt if using. Reduce heat to low and simmer, stirring occasionally, for about 5-7 minutes or until the oats are tender and have absorbed most of the liquid.
3. If using cinnamon, stir it in during the last minute of cooking.
4. While the oatmeal is cooking, wash and slice the berries.
5. If you prefer a sweeter oatmeal, drizzle honey or maple syrup over the berries.
6. Divide the cooked oatmeal between two bowls.
7. Top each bowl with fresh blueberries, strawberries, and raspberries.
8. Sprinkle with chia seeds or flaxseeds if desired.

Nutrition: Cal 400; Fat 20g; Carb 30g; Protein 25g

BREAKFAST

2 serving

10 minutes

10 minutes

Spinach Omelette

Ingredients

- 4 large eggs
- 1 cup fresh spinach, chopped
- 1/4 cup onion, finely chopped
- 1/4 cup bell pepper, finely chopped (optional)
- 1/4 cup shredded cheese (such as feta, cheddar, or mozzarella) (optional)
- 1 tbsp olive oil or butter
- Salt and black pepper to taste

Optional Garnishes:
- Fresh herbs (such as parsley or chives), chopped
- Sliced avocado

Instructions

1. Wash and chop the spinach.
2. Finely chop the onion and bell pepper if using.
3. Heat the olive oil or butter in a non-stick skillet over medium heat.
4. Add the chopped onion and bell pepper (if using) and sauté for about 2-3 minutes until softened.
5. Add the chopped spinach and cook for another 1-2 minutes until wilted. Remove the vegetables from the skillet and set aside.
6. In a bowl, whisk the eggs with a pinch of salt and pepper until well blended.
7. Pour the eggs into the same skillet over medium heat. Let them cook undisturbed for about 1-2 minutes until the edges start to set.
8. Spread the cooked vegetables evenly over one half of the omelette.
9. If using cheese, sprinkle it on top of the vegetables.
10. Once the eggs are mostly set but still a bit runny on top, use a spatula to gently fold the omelette in half over the filling.
11. Cook for another 1-2 minutes until the eggs are fully set and the cheese is melted (if using).
12. Slide the omelette onto a plate and garnish with fresh herbs and avocado slices if desired.

Nutrition: Cal 250; Fat 20g; Carb 5g; Protein 15g

BREAKFAST
2 serving
0 minutes
15 minutes

Oat and Berry Acai Bowl

Ingredients

- 1 packet (100g) frozen acai puree (unsweetened or lightly sweetened)
- 1/2 cup rolled oats
- 1/2 cup unsweetened almond milk (or any plant-based milk)
- 1 banana, sliced
- 1/2 cup fresh or frozen berries (such as strawberries, blueberries, or raspberries)

For Toppings:
- 1/4 cup granola (low-sugar variety)
- 2 tbsp chia seeds or flaxseeds
- Fresh berries (strawberries, blueberries, raspberries)
- Sliced banana
- A drizzle of honey or maple syrup (optional)

Instructions

1. In a blender, combine the frozen acai puree with the almond milk. Blend until smooth. If the mixture is too thick, you can add a bit more almond milk to reach your desired consistency.

2. In a small bowl, combine the rolled oats with a bit of almond milk (just enough to cover the oats). Let it sit for about 10 minutes or until the oats absorb the liquid and become slightly soft. Alternatively, you can cook the oats on the stove or in the microwave according to package instructions if you prefer them warm.

3. Divide the acai mixture evenly between two bowls.

4. Add a layer of the prepared oats on top of the acai base.

5. Arrange fresh berries, sliced banana, and granola on top of the oats and acai mixture.

6. Sprinkle with chia seeds or flaxseeds for added texture and nutrients.

7. Drizzle with a small amount of honey or maple syrup if desired for extra sweetness.

Nutrition: Cal 350; Fat 10g; Carb 50g; Protein 7g

BREAKFAST

2 serving

10 minutes

10 minutes

Avocado and Poached Egg Sandwich

Ingredients

- 2 slices of whole-grain or sprouted bread (preferably low-carb and high in fiber)
- 1 ripe avocado
- 2 large eggs
- 1 tbsp white vinegar (for poaching eggs)
- 1 small tomato, sliced
- A handful of fresh spinach or arugula
- Salt and pepper, to taste
- Optional: red pepper flakes or hot sauce for extra flavor

Instructions

1. Cut the avocado in half, remove the pit, and scoop the flesh into a small bowl.
2. Mash the avocado with a fork until smooth. Season with salt and pepper to taste. You can also add a squeeze of lemon juice for extra flavor and freshness if desired.
3. Fill a medium saucepan with about 2-3 inches of water. Add the white vinegar and bring to a gentle simmer over medium heat.
4. Crack each egg into a small bowl or cup, being careful not to break the yolk.
5. Create a gentle whirlpool in the simmering water using a spoon. Carefully slide one egg into the center of the whirlpool. Repeat with the second egg.
6. Poach the eggs for about 3-4 minutes, or until the whites are set and the yolks are still soft. Remove the eggs with a slotted spoon and gently drain on a paper towel.
7. Toast the bread slices to your desired level of crispness. You can use a toaster or a skillet.
8. Spread the mashed avocado evenly on one side of each slice of toasted bread.
9. Top one slice with fresh spinach or arugula, tomato slices, and the poached egg.
10. Season with additional salt, pepper, and optional red pepper flakes or hot sauce.
11. Place the other slice of toast on top to complete the sandwich.
12. Cut the sandwich in half if desired and serve immediately.

Nutrition: Cal   350;   Fat   20g;   Carb   30g;   Protein   20g

2 serving

20 minutes

10 minutes

BREAKFAST

Green Shakshuka

Ingredients

- 2 tbsp olive oil
- 1 small onion, finely chopped
- 3 cloves garlic, minced
- 1 cup spinach leaves (fresh or frozen, thawed)
- 1 cup kale leaves, stems removed
- 1/2 cup fresh cilantro
- 1/2 cup fresh parsley
- 1 cup green bell pepper, diced
- 1/2 cup green tomatoes or regular tomatoes, diced
- 1/2 tsp ground cumin
- 1/2 tsp ground coriander
- 1/2 tsp dried oregano
- Salt and black pepper, to taste

For the Poached Eggs:
- 4 large eggs
- 1 tbsp white vinegar (for poaching)

Instructions

1. Heat olive oil in a large skillet or cast-iron pan over medium heat.
2. Add the chopped onion and cook until it becomes translucent, about 5 minutes.
3. Add the minced garlic and cook for an additional 1-2 minutes until fragrant.
4. Stir in the diced green bell pepper and cook for another 5 minutes, until softened.
5. Add the spinach, kale, cilantro, and parsley. Cook until the greens are wilted, about 3-4 minutes.
6. Add the diced tomatoes, ground cumin, ground coriander, dried oregano, salt, and black pepper. Stir to combine.
7. Simmer the sauce for 5-10 minutes, allowing the flavors to meld together. You can use an immersion blender to slightly blend the sauce if desired, but it should still have some texture.
8. While the sauce is simmering, fill a medium saucepan with about 2-3 inches of water and add the white vinegar. Bring to a gentle simmer over medium heat.
9. Crack each egg into a small bowl or cup. Carefully slide one egg into the simmering water. Repeat with the remaining eggs.
10. Poach the eggs for about 3-4 minutes, or until the whites are set and the yolks are still runny. Use a slotted spoon to remove the eggs from the water and drain them on a paper towel.
11. Create small wells in the simmering green sauce using a spoon.
12. Gently place a poached egg into each well.
13. Cover the skillet with a lid and let the eggs sit in the sauce for a minute to warm through, if needed.
14. Garnish with additional fresh herbs or a sprinkle of crumbled feta cheese if desired.
15. Serve immediately, optionally with a side of whole-grain toast or a light salad.

Nutrition: Cal 250; Fat 15g; Carb 15g; Protein 15g

BREAKFAST

2 serving

15 minutes

10 minutes

Baked Eggs in Avocado

Ingredients

- 1 ripe avocado
- 2 large eggs
- Salt and black pepper, to taste
- Optional toppings: chopped fresh herbs (like chives or parsley), crumbled feta cheese, paprika, or hot sauce

Instructions

1. Preheat your oven to 425°F (220°C).
2. Cut the avocado in half lengthwise and remove the pit.
3. If the avocado's indent where the pit was is too small to hold an egg, gently scoop out a little extra flesh to create more space.
4. Place the avocado halves in a small baking dish or on a baking sheet. You may want to use a spoon or a small crumpled piece of aluminum foil under the avocado halves to keep them stable and level.
5. Crack an egg into a small dish, then carefully slip the egg into the hollowed-out center of one avocado half. Repeat with the second avocado half.
6. Be careful not to overfill; you may need to discard some of the egg white if it overflows.
7. Season the eggs with salt and black pepper.
8. Bake in the preheated oven for 12-15 minutes, or until the egg whites are set but the yolks are still slightly runny. For firmer yolks, bake for an additional 2-3 minutes.
9. If desired, sprinkle with fresh herbs, crumbled feta cheese, paprika, or a dash of hot sauce before serving.

Nutrition: : Cal 250; Fat 20g; Carb 12g; Protein 12g

2 serving

10 minutes

10 minutes

BREAKFAST

Coconut Flour Pancakes with Berries

Ingredients

- 1/4 cup coconut flour
- 1/4 tsp baking powder
- 2 eggs
- 1/4 cup almond milk
- 1 tbsp coconut oil, melted
- 1/2 tsp vanilla extract
- 1/2 cup mixed berries (blueberries, raspberries, strawberries)
- 1 tbsp honey or maple syrup (optional, for serving)

Instructions

1. In a mixing bowl, combine the coconut flour and baking powder.
2. In another bowl, whisk together the eggs, almond milk, melted coconut oil, and vanilla extract.
3. Gradually add the wet ingredients to the dry ingredients, stirring until smooth. Let the batter sit for a few minutes to thicken.
4. Heat a non-stick skillet or griddle over medium heat and lightly grease with coconut oil.
5. Pour small amounts of batter (about 2-3 tbsps) onto the skillet for each pancake.
6. Cook for 2-3 minutes, or until bubbles start to form on the surface. Flip and cook for another 1-2 minutes on the other side, until golden brown and cooked through.
7. Top the pancakes with mixed berries and drizzle with honey or maple syrup, if desired.

Nutrition: Cal 320; Fat 22g; Carb 20g; Protein 12g

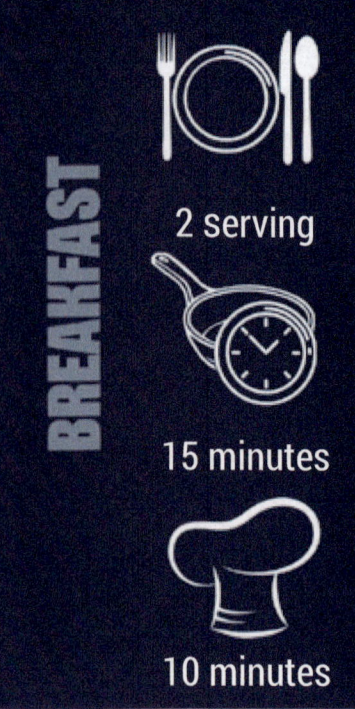

BREAKFAST

2 serving

15 minutes

10 minutes

Sweet Potato and Spinach Breakfast Hash

Ingredients

- 1 medium sweet potato, diced
- 2 cups fresh spinach
- 1 small onion, chopped
- 2 eggs
- 2 tbsp olive oil
- Salt and pepper to taste

Instructions

1. Heat 1 tbsp of olive oil in a large skillet over medium heat.
2. Add the diced sweet potato and cook, stirring occasionally, for about 10-12 minutes, or until the sweet potato is tender and slightly crispy.
3. Add the chopped onion to the skillet with the sweet potato. Cook for an additional 3-4 minutes until the onion is translucent and fragrant.
4. Add the fresh spinach to the skillet. Cook, stirring, until the spinach is wilted, about 1-2 minutes. Season with salt and pepper to taste.
5. Push the sweet potato and spinach mixture to one side of the skillet.
6. Add the remaining 1 tbsp of olive oil to the vacant side of the skillet. Crack the eggs into the skillet and cook to your desired doneness (sunny side up, over easy, etc.).
7. Divide the sweet potato and spinach hash between plates. Top each serving with a cooked egg. Season with additional salt and pepper if desired.

Nutrition: Cal 310; Fat 22g; Carb 27g; Protein 12g

2 serving

25 minutes

15 minutes

LUNCH

Almond Chicken with Broccoli

Ingredients

- 2 boneless, skinless chicken breasts (about 1 pound total)
- 1/2 cup almond flour
- 1/4 cup grated Parmesan cheese (optional, for extra flavor)
- 1/2 tsp garlic powder
- 1/2 tsp onion powder
- 1/4 tsp paprika
- Salt and black pepper, to taste
- 2 tbsp olive oil (for cooking)

For the Broccoli:
- 2 cups broccoli florets
- 1 tbsp olive oil
- 1 clove garlic, minced
- Salt and black pepper, to taste
- 2 tbsp sliced almonds (for garnish)

Instructions

1. Preheat the oven to 375°F (190°C).
2. In a shallow dish, mix almond flour, grated Parmesan cheese (if using), garlic powder, onion powder, paprika, salt, and black pepper.
3. Dredge each chicken breast in the almond flour mixture, coating evenly.
4. Heat olive oil in a large oven-safe skillet over medium-high heat. Add the coated chicken breasts and cook for about 3-4 minutes per side, or until golden brown.
5. Transfer the skillet to the preheated oven and bake for 15-20 minutes, or until the chicken is cooked through (internal temperature should reach 165°F or 74°C).
6. While the chicken is baking, heat olive oil in a large skillet over medium heat.
7. Add minced garlic and cook for about 1 minute, or until fragrant.
8. Add broccoli florets to the skillet and sauté for 5-7 minutes or until tender-crisp. Season with salt and black pepper.
9. Stir in sliced almonds and cook for an additional 1-2 minutes.
10. Slice the baked chicken breasts and serve alongside the sautéed broccoli.
11. Garnish with additional sliced almonds if desired.

Nutrition: Cal 400; Fat 28g; Carb 15g; Protein 30g

LUNCH
2 serving
35 minutes
15 minutes

Stuffed Bell Peppers with Ground Beef and Quinoa

Ingredients

- 2 large bell peppers (any color)
- 1/2 cup quinoa, rinsed
- 1 cup water or low-sodium chicken broth
- 1/2 pound ground beef (preferably lean)
- 1 small onion, finely chopped
- 2 cloves garlic, minced
- 1/2 cup diced tomatoes (fresh or canned)
- 1/2 tsp dried oregano
- 1/2 tsp dried basil
- 1/4 tsp paprika
- Salt and black pepper, to taste
- 1/4 cup shredded cheese (optional, such as cheddar or mozzarella)
- Fresh parsley or basil, chopped (optional)

Instructions

1. Preheat the oven to 375°F (190°C).
2. In a small saucepan, bring 1 cup of water or chicken broth to a boil. Add the rinsed quinoa, reduce heat to low, cover, and simmer for 15 minutes, or until quinoa is cooked and water is absorbed. Fluff with a fork and set aside.
3. Cut the tops off the bell peppers and remove seeds and membranes.
4. Place the peppers cut-side up in a baking dish.
5. Heat a large skillet over medium heat. Add the ground beef and cook until browned, breaking it up with a spoon as it cooks.
6. Add the chopped onion and minced garlic to the skillet and cook until the onion is translucent.
7. Stir in the diced tomatoes, oregano, basil, paprika, salt, and black pepper. Cook for another 2-3 minutes.
8. Add the cooked quinoa to the skillet and mix well to combine.
9. Spoon the beef and quinoa mixture into the bell peppers, packing it in lightly.
10. If using cheese, sprinkle the shredded cheese on top of the stuffed peppers.
11. Cover the baking dish with aluminum foil and bake in the preheated oven for 25-30 minutes or until the peppers are tender.
12. Remove the foil and bake for an additional 5 minutes if you want the cheese to be melted and slightly browned.
13. Garnish with fresh parsley or basil if desired.

Nutrition: Cal 350; Fat 15g; Carb 30g; Protein 22g

2 serving

15 minutes

10 minutes

LUNCH

Zoodles with Pesto Sauce and Turkey

Ingredients

For the Zoodles:
- 2 medium zucchinis
- 1 tbsp olive oil
- Salt and pepper to taste

For the Pesto Sauce:
- 1 cup fresh basil leaves
- 1/4 cup pine nuts (or walnuts)
- 1/4 cup grated Parmesan cheese
- 1/4 cup extra-virgin olive oil
- 2 cloves garlic
- Salt and pepper to taste

For the Turkey:
- 1/2 pound ground turkey
- 1 small onion, finely chopped
- 2 cloves garlic, minced
- 1 tbsp olive oil
- Salt and pepper to taste

Instructions

1. Use a spiralizer to create zucchini noodles (zoodles) from the zucchinis.
2. Heat 1 tbsp of olive oil in a large skillet over medium heat.
3. Add the zoodles to the skillet and cook for 2-3 minutes, stirring occasionally, until tender. Season with salt and pepper. Remove from heat and set aside.
4. In a food processor, combine basil leaves, pine nuts, Parmesan cheese, garlic, and a pinch of salt and pepper.
5. With the food processor running, slowly stream in the olive oil until the pesto is smooth and well combined. Adjust seasoning to taste.
6. Heat 1 tbsp of olive oil in a skillet over medium heat.
7. Add the chopped onion and garlic and cook until the onion is translucent.
8. Add the ground turkey, breaking it up with a spoon. Cook until the turkey is browned and cooked through. Season with salt and pepper.
9. Toss the cooked zoodles with the pesto sauce until well coated.
10. Serve the zoodles topped with the cooked turkey.

Nutrition: Cal 350; Fat 24g; Carb 12g; Protein 27g

LUNCH
2 serving
20 minutes
10 minutes

Mushroom Cream Soup

Ingredients

- 2 cups mushrooms, sliced (e.g., cremini or button mushrooms)
- 1 tbsp olive oil
- 1 small onion, finely chopped
- 2 cloves garlic, minced
- 2 cups low-sodium vegetable or chicken broth
- 1/2 cup full-fat coconut milk (or heavy cream)
- 1 tsp fresh thyme leaves (or 1/2 tsp dried thyme)
- Salt and black pepper to taste

For Garnish:
- Fresh parsley, chopped (optional)
- A drizzle of olive oil (optional)

Instructions

1. Heat 1 tbsp of olive oil in a medium pot over medium heat.
2. Add the chopped onion and cook until translucent, about 3-4 minutes.
3. Add the minced garlic and cook for an additional 1 minute until fragrant.
4. Add the sliced mushrooms to the pot and cook until they are softened and lightly browned, about 5-7 minutes.
5. Pour in the vegetable or chicken broth and add the thyme.
6. Bring the mixture to a simmer and cook for 10 minutes, allowing the flavors to meld.
7. Use an immersion blender to blend the soup until smooth. Alternatively, you can carefully transfer the soup to a blender in batches and blend until smooth.
8. Return the blended soup to the pot (if you used a regular blender).
9. Stir in the coconut milk (or heavy cream) and cook for an additional 2-3 minutes until heated through. Adjust seasoning with salt and pepper to taste.
10. Ladle the soup into bowls and garnish with chopped parsley and a drizzle of olive oil if desired.

Nutrition: Cal 200; Fat 16g; Carb 10g; Protein 4g

2 serving

20 minutes

10 minutes

LUNCH

Broccoli and Cheese Cream Soup

Ingredients

- 2 cups broccoli florets (about 1 small head of broccoli)
- 1 tbsp olive oil
- 1 small onion, chopped
- 2 cloves garlic, minced
- 2 cups low-sodium vegetable or chicken broth
- 1/2 cup full-fat coconut milk (or heavy cream)
- 1/2 cup shredded cheddar cheese (or other preferred cheese)
- 0.5 teaspoon of dehydrated thyme (or 1 teaspoon of fresh thyme)
- Salt and black pepper to taste

For Garnish:
- Fresh parsley, chopped (optional)
- A drizzle of olive oil (optional)

Instructions

1. Steam or blanch the broccoli florets until tender, about 5 minutes. You can also cook them directly in the pot with a bit of broth if you prefer.
2. Heat olive oil in a medium pot over medium heat.
3. Add the chopped onion and cook until translucent, about 3-4 minutes.
4. Add minced garlic and cook for another minute until fragrant.
5. Add the steamed or blanched broccoli florets to the pot with the onions and garlic.
6. Pour in the vegetable or chicken broth.
7. Bring to a simmer and cook for 5-7 minutes.
8. Use an immersion blender to blend the soup until smooth. Alternatively, carefully transfer the soup to a blender in batches and blend until smooth.
9. Return the blended soup to the pot if using a regular blender.
10. Stir in the coconut milk (or heavy cream) and shredded cheese.
11. Cook for an additional 2-3 minutes, stirring until the cheese is fully melted and the soup is heated through.
12. Season with dried thyme, salt, and black pepper to taste.
13. Ladle the soup into bowls and garnish with extra shredded cheese and chopped parsley if desired

Nutrition: Cal 250; Fat 20g; Carb 12g; Protein 10g

LUNCH
2 serving
30 minutes
15 minutes

Vegetable and Nut Stew

Ingredients

- 1 tbsp olive oil
- 1 small onion, chopped
- 2 cloves garlic, minced
- 1 cup carrots, diced
- 1 cup celery, diced
- 1 cup bell peppers, diced
- 1 cup zucchini, diced
- 1 cup green beans, cut into 1-inch pieces
- 1 cup diced tomatoes (canned or fresh)
- 2 cups low-sodium vegetable or chicken broth
- 1/2 cup raw cashews or almonds, chopped (or other preferred nuts)
- 0.5 teaspoon of dehydrated thyme (or 1 teaspoon of fresh thyme)
- 1/2 tsp dried rosemary
- Salt and black pepper to taste

For Garnish:
- Fresh parsley, chopped (optional)

Instructions

1. Heat olive oil in a large pot over medium heat.
2. Add the chopped onion and cook until translucent, about 3-4 minutes.
3. Add minced garlic and cook for an additional minute until fragrant.
4. Add the diced carrots, celery, bell peppers, zucchini, and green beans to the pot.
5. Sauté for 5-7 minutes, stirring occasionally, until the vegetables start to soften.
6. Stir in the diced tomatoes and cook for another 2 minutes.
7. Pour in the vegetable or chicken broth and bring to a simmer.
8. Reduce heat and let the stew simmer for 15-20 minutes or until all vegetables are tender.
9. Stir in the chopped nuts and cook for an additional 5 minutes.
10. Add dried thyme, dried rosemary, salt, and black pepper to taste.
11. Adjust seasoning as needed.
12. Ladle the stew into bowls. Garnish with fresh parsley and extra chopped nuts if desired.

Nutrition: Cal 300; Fat 20g; Carb 20g; Protein 8g

2 serving

30 minutes

15 minutes

LUNCH

Red Lentil and Chicken Stew

Ingredients

- 1 tbsp olive oil
- 1 small onion, chopped
- 2 cloves garlic, minced
- 1 cup carrots, diced
- 1 cup celery, diced
- 1 cup bell peppers, diced
- 1/2 cup red lentils, rinsed
- 1 cup diced tomatoes (canned or fresh)
- 2 cups low-sodium chicken broth
- 1 cup cooked chicken breast, shredded or diced
- 1 tsp dried thyme
- 1/2 tsp dried rosemary
- 1/2 tsp ground cumin
- Salt and black pepper to taste

For Garnish:
- Fresh parsley, chopped (optional)
- A drizzle of olive oil (optional)

Instructions

1. Heat olive oil in a large pot over medium heat.
2. Add the chopped onion and cook until translucent, about 3-4 minutes.
3. Add minced garlic and cook for an additional minute until fragrant.
4. Add the diced carrots, celery, and bell peppers to the pot.
5. Sauté for 5-7 minutes, stirring occasionally, until the vegetables start to soften.
6. Stir in the rinsed red lentils and diced tomatoes.
7. Cook for 2 minutes, stirring occasionally.
8. Pour in the chicken broth and bring to a simmer.
9. Reduce heat and let the stew simmer for 15-20 minutes, or until the lentils and vegetables are tender.
10. Stir in the cooked chicken breast.
11. Add dried thyme, dried rosemary, ground cumin, salt, and black pepper.
12. Simmer for an additional 5 minutes to heat the chicken through and meld the flavors.
13. Ladle the stew into bowls. Garnish with fresh parsley and serve with lemon wedges if desired.

Nutrition: Cal 350; Fat 10g; Carb 235g; Protein 25g

LUNCH
2 serving
0 minutes
10 minutes

Mediterranean Chickpea Salad

Ingredients

- 1 can (15 ounces) chickpeas, drained and rinsed
- 1 cucumber, diced
- 1 cup cherry tomatoes, halved
- 1/2 cup diced red onion
- 1/2 cup chopped fresh parsley
- 4 tbsp olive oil
- 2 tbsp lemon juice
- Salt and pepper to taste

Instructions

1. In a large mixing bowl, combine the chickpeas, diced cucumber, halved cherry tomatoes, diced red onion, and chopped fresh parsley.
2. In a small bowl, whisk together the olive oil and lemon juice to make the dressing. Season with salt and pepper to taste.
3. Pour the dressing over the chickpea mixture and toss until well coated.
4. Divide the Mediterranean chickpea salad into two equal portions.
5. Serve immediately, or refrigerate for about 30 minutes to allow the flavors to meld together before serving.

Nutrition: Cal 360; Fat 21g; Carb 38g; Protein 10g

2 serving

0 minutes

15 minutes

LUNCH

Quinoa and Black Bean Salad

Ingredients

- 2 cups cooked quinoa
- 1 can (15 ounces) black beans, drained and rinsed
- 1 bell pepper, diced
- 1/2 cup chopped fresh cilantro
- 4 tbsp lime juice
- 4 tbsp olive oil
- Salt and pepper to taste

Instructions

1. In a large mixing bowl, combine the cooked quinoa, black beans, diced bell pepper, and chopped fresh cilantro.
2. In a small bowl, whisk together the lime juice and olive oil to make the dressing. Season with salt and pepper to taste.
3. Pour the dressing over the quinoa and black bean mixture, and toss until well-combined and evenly coated.
4. Divide the quinoa and black bean salad into two equal portions.
5. Serve immediately, or refrigerate for about 30 minutes to allow the flavors to meld together before serving.

Nutrition: Cal 420; Fat 19g; Carb 51g; Protein 14g

LUNCH
2 serving
0 minutes
15 minutes

Shrimp Avocado Salad

Ingredients

- 1 pound cooked shrimp, peeled and deveined
- 2 avocados, diced
- 2 cups cherry tomatoes, halved
- 1/2 cup chopped fresh cilantro
- 4 tbsp lime juice
- 2 tbsp olive oil
- Salt and pepper to taste

Instructions

1. In a large mixing bowl, combine the cooked shrimp, diced avocados, halved cherry tomatoes, and chopped fresh cilantro.
2. In a small bowl, whisk together the lime juice, olive oil, salt, and pepper to make the dressing.
3. Pour the dressing over the shrimp and avocado mixture, and toss gently until all ingredients are evenly coated.
4. Serve the shrimp avocado salad immediately, or refrigerate for about 30 minutes to allow the flavors to meld together before serving.

Nutrition: Cal   450;   Fat   30g;   Carb   21g;   Protein   30g

2 serving

0 minutes

10 minutes

LUNCH

Tuna and White Bean Salad

Ingredients

- 2 cans (15 ounces each) white beans, drained and rinsed
- 2 cans (5 ounces each) tuna, drained
- 1/2 cup diced red onion
- 1/2 cup chopped fresh parsley
- 4 tbsp olive oil
- 2 tbsp lemon juice
- Salt and pepper to taste

Instructions

1. In a large mixing bowl, combine the white beans, tuna, diced red onion, and chopped fresh parsley.
2. In a small bowl, whisk together the olive oil, lemon juice, salt, and pepper to make the dressing.
3. Pour the dressing over the tuna and white bean mixture, and toss gently until all ingredients are evenly coated.
4. Serve the tuna and white bean salad immediately, or refrigerate for about 30 minutes to allow the flavors to meld together before serving.

Nutrition: Cal 420; Fat 17g; Carb 37g; Protein 34g

LUNCH
2 serving
0 minutes
10 minutes

Avocado and Turkey Wrap

Ingredients

- 2 whole grain tortillas
- 6 slices turkey breast
- 1 avocado, sliced
- Handful of baby spinach leaves
- 1 small tomato, sliced

For the Greek Yogurt Dressing:
- 1/2 cup plain Greek yogurt
- 2 tbsp lemon juice
- 2 tsp Dijon mustard
- 1 tsp honey
- Salt and pepper to taste

Instructions

For the Greek Yogurt Dressing:
1. In a small bowl, combine the plain Greek yogurt, lemon juice, Dijon mustard, honey, salt, and pepper. Whisk until smooth and well combined. Adjust seasoning to taste.

For the Avocado and Turkey Wrap:
2. Lay out the whole grain tortillas on a clean surface.
3. Divide the sliced turkey breast, sliced avocado, baby spinach leaves, and sliced tomato equally between the two tortillas, arranging them in the center of each tortilla.
4. Drizzle the Greek yogurt dressing over the ingredients on each tortilla.
5. Fold in the sides of each tortilla, then roll them up tightly from the bottom to form wraps.

Nutrition: Cal 450; Fat 30g; Carb 21g; Protein 30g

2 serving

0 minutes

10 minutes

LUNCH

Cheeseburger Lettuce Sliders

Ingredients

- 6 ounces ground beef
- Salt and black pepper
- 1 tbsp olive oil
- 4 large bibb or romaine lettuce leaves
- 2 slices cheddar cheese
- 2 tbsp olive oil mayonnaise
- 2 slices ripe tomato
- 1 avocado, sliced
- 4 small onion slices
- 2 slices dill pickle

Instructions

1. Divide the ground beef into two equal portions and shape them into patties. Season both sides of each patty with salt and black pepper.
2. Heat olive oil in a skillet over medium-high heat. Cook the beef patties for about 3-4 minutes on each side or until they reach your desired level of doneness.
3. While the patties are cooking, arrange the lettuce leaves on a clean surface.
4. Place a slice of cheddar cheese on top of each lettuce leaf.
5. Once the beef patties are cooked, place them on top of the cheese-covered lettuce leaves.
6. Spread olive oil mayonnaise on each patty.
7. Top each patty with a slice of ripe tomato, avocado slices, onion slices, and a dill pickle slice.
8. Fold the sides of each lettuce leaf over the toppings to form sliders.

Nutrition: Cal   530;   Fat   41g;   Carb   9g;   Protein   31g

LUNCH
2 serving
25 minutes
15 minutes

Lemon Garlic Turkey Meatballs with Green Beans

Ingredients

- 1 pound ground turkey
- 1/4 cup finely chopped fresh parsley
- 2 cloves garlic, minced
- 1 tbsp lemon zest
- 1 tbsp lemon juice
- 1/2 tsp dried oregano
- 1/2 tsp dried thyme
- 1/4 cup almond flour
- 1 large egg
- Salt and black pepper to taste

For the Green Beans:

- 2 cups fresh green beans, trimmed
- 1 tbsp olive oil
- 1 clove garlic, minced
- Salt and black pepper to taste
- Lemon zest (optional, for garnish)

Instructions

1. Preheat the oven to 375°F (190°C) and line a baking sheet with parchment paper.
2. In a large bowl, combine ground turkey, parsley, minced garlic, lemon zest, lemon juice, dried oregano, dried thyme, almond flour, egg, salt, and black pepper.
3. Mix until well combined but avoid over-mixing to keep the meatballs tender.
4. Shape the mixture into 12-15 meatballs and place them on the prepared baking sheet.
5. Bake in the preheated oven for 20-25 minutes, or until the meatballs are cooked through and have an internal temperature of 165°F (74°C).
6. While the meatballs are baking, heat olive oil in a large skillet over medium heat.
7. Add minced garlic and sauté for about 1 minute until fragrant.
8. Add the green beans to the skillet and season with salt and black pepper.
9. Cook the green beans, stirring occasionally, for 5-7 minutes or until they are tender yet still crisp. You can cover the skillet with a lid to steam the beans slightly for quicker cooking.
10. Arrange the cooked meatballs and green beans on plates.
11. Optionally, garnish the green beans with additional lemon zest for extra flavor.

Nutrition: Cal 380; Fat 18g; Carb 20g; Protein 30g

2 serving

25 minutes

15 minutes

LUNCH

Chicken Casserole with Broccoli

Ingredients

- 1 pound boneless, skinless chicken breasts or thighs, diced
- 2 cups fresh broccoli florets
- 1/2 cup plain Greek yogurt
- 1/4 cup grated Parmesan cheese
- 1/4 cup almond flour
- 1/4 cup chicken broth (low sodium)
- 2 cloves garlic, minced
- 1 tsp dried thyme
- 1 tsp dried oregano
- Salt and black pepper to taste
- 1 tbsp olive oil

For Topping (optional):

- 1/4 cup shredded cheddar cheese (or more Parmesan cheese)
- Fresh parsley, chopped (for garnish)

Instructions

1. Preheat your oven to 375°F (190°C) and lightly grease a baking dish.
2. Heat olive oil in a large skillet over medium heat.
3. Add the diced chicken and cook until browned and cooked through, about 5-7 minutes. Season with salt and black pepper.
4. Remove the chicken from the skillet and set aside.
5. In the same skillet, add a little more olive oil if needed and sauté the minced garlic until fragrant, about 1 minute.
6. Add the broccoli florets and cook for about 3-4 minutes until slightly tender. The broccoli will continue to cook in the oven, so it doesn't need to be fully cooked at this stage.
7. In a mixing bowl, combine Greek yogurt, Parmesan cheese, almond flour, chicken broth, dried thyme, dried oregano, salt, and black pepper. Mix until well combined.
8. Add the cooked chicken and broccoli to the bowl and stir to coat everything evenly with the yogurt mixture.
9. Transfer the mixture to the prepared baking dish.
10. Sprinkle shredded cheddar cheese or additional Parmesan cheese on top of the casserole.
11. Bake in the preheated oven for 20-25 minutes, or until the casserole is bubbly and the top is golden brown.
12. Garnish with chopped fresh parsley if desired. Serve hot.

Nutrition: Cal 360; Fat 20g; Carb 16g; Protein 30g

LUNCH
2 serving
30 minutes
20 minutes

Chicken Breast Stuffed Spinach and Cheese with Boiled Vegetables

Ingredients

- 2 boneless, skinless chicken breasts
- 1 cup fresh spinach, chopped
- 1/2 cup shredded mozzarella cheese (or another cheese like feta or goat cheese)
- 1 tbsp olive oil
- 1 garlic clove, minced
- 1/4 tsp dried thyme
- 1/4 tsp dried oregano
- Salt and black pepper to taste
- Toothpicks or kitchen twine

For the Boiled Vegetables:

- 1 cup carrots, peeled and sliced
- 1 cup green beans, trimmed
- 1 cup broccoli florets
- Salt and pepper to taste
- Optional: a splash of lemon juice or a drizzle of olive oil for seasoning

Instructions

1. Preheat your oven to 375°F (190°C).
2. Place the chicken breasts between two sheets of plastic wrap or parchment paper. Gently pound with a meat mallet or rolling pin until they are even in thickness (about 1/2 inch thick).
3. Season the chicken breasts with salt and pepper on both sides.
4. In a skillet, heat olive oil over medium heat.
5. Add minced garlic and cook until fragrant, about 1 minute.
6. Add chopped spinach and cook until wilted and any excess moisture has evaporated, about 2-3 minutes. Remove from heat and let cool slightly.
7. Stir in the shredded cheese and dried thyme and oregano. Mix until well combined.
8. Spoon the spinach and cheese mixture evenly onto one side of each chicken breast.
9. Fold the other side of the chicken over the filling and secure with toothpicks or tie with kitchen twine to hold the stuffing inside.
10. Place the stuffed chicken breasts in a baking dish.
11. Bake in the preheated oven for 25-30 minutes, or until the chicken is cooked through and reaches an internal temperature of 165°F (74°C).
12. Remove the toothpicks or twine before serving.
13. While the chicken is baking, bring a large pot of salted water to a boil.
14. Add the carrots, green beans, and broccoli. Cook until tender, about 5-7 minutes.
15. Drain the vegetables and season with salt and pepper. Optionally, add a splash of lemon juice or a drizzle of olive oil.
16. Serve the stuffed chicken breasts hot with the boiled vegetables on the side.

Nutrition: Cal 360; Fat 18g; Carb 15g; Protein 40g

2 serving

20 minutes

10 minutes

DINNER

Salmon and Asparagus Foil Packets

Ingredients

- 2 salmon fillets (about 6 ounces each)
- 1 bunch asparagus, trimmed
- 2 tbsp lemon juice
- 2 tbsp olive oil
- 1 tsp dried dill
- Salt and pepper to taste

Instructions

1. Preheat your oven to 400°F (200°C).
2. Cut two large pieces of aluminum foil, each about 12 inches long.
3. Place a salmon fillet in the center of each piece of foil.
4. Arrange the trimmed asparagus around the salmon fillets.
5. In a small bowl, mix the lemon juice, olive oil, dried dill, salt, and pepper.
6. Drizzle the mixture evenly over the salmon and asparagus.
7. Overlap the edges of the foil over the salmon and asparagus, creating a sealed packet. Ensure the packets are well-sealed to trap the steam.
8. Place the foil packets on a baking sheet and bake in the preheated oven for 20-25 minutes, or until the salmon is cooked through and flakes easily with a fork, and the asparagus is tender.
9. Carefully open the foil packets (watch out for steam) and transfer the salmon and asparagus to plates.

Nutrition: Cal 350; Fat 22g; Carb 8g; Protein 34g

DINNER

2 serving

35 minutes

10 minutes

Baked Chicken with Brussels Sprouts

Ingredients

- 2 chicken thighs, bone-in and skin-on or boneless and skinless
- 1 cup Brussels sprouts, halved
- 1 tbsp olive oil
- 1 clove garlic, minced
- 1 tsp dried thyme
- Salt and pepper to taste

Instructions

1. Preheat your oven to 400°F (200°C).
2. Pat the chicken thighs dry with paper towels. Season both sides with salt, pepper, and dried thyme.
3. In a large bowl, toss the halved Brussels sprouts with olive oil, minced garlic, salt, and pepper.
4. Place the seasoned chicken thighs in the center of a baking dish or a rimmed baking sheet.
5. Arrange the Brussels sprouts around the chicken, ensuring they are evenly spread out.
6. Bake in the preheated oven for 30-35 minutes, or until the chicken reaches an internal temperature of 165°F (74°C) and the Brussels sprouts are tender and caramelized. If using bone-in chicken thighs, ensure the meat is cooked through and the skin is crispy.
7. Let the chicken rest for a few minutes before serving. Serve with the roasted Brussels sprouts.

Nutrition: Cal 320; Fat 20g; Carb 12g; Protein 26g

2 serving

25 minutes

10 minutes

DINNER

Stuffed Zucchini Boats

Ingredients

- 2 medium zucchinis, halved lengthwise
- 1/2 cup ground turkey
- 1/4 cup diced tomatoes
- 1/4 cup chopped onion
- 1 clove garlic, minced
- 1/4 cup grated Parmesan cheese
- Salt and pepper to taste
- 1 tbsp olive oil (optional, for sautéing)

Instructions

1. Preheat your oven to 375°F (190°C).
2. Use a spoon to scoop out the seeds from the center of each zucchini half, creating a hollow space for stuffing. Place the zucchini halves in a baking dish.
3. In a skillet over medium heat, add the olive oil (if using). Sauté the chopped onion and minced garlic until softened, about 2-3 minutes.
4. Add the ground turkey to the skillet and cook until browned and cooked through, breaking it up with a spoon as it cooks.
5. Stir in the diced tomatoes and cook for another 2 minutes. Season with salt and pepper to taste.
6. Spoon the turkey mixture evenly into the hollowed-out zucchini halves.
7. Sprinkle the grated Parmesan cheese on top of each stuffed zucchini boat.
8. Bake in the preheated oven for 20-25 minutes, or until the zucchini is tender and the cheese is melted and golden brown.
9. Let the zucchini boats cool slightly before serving.

Nutrition: Cal 230; Fat 12g; Carb 10g; Protein 22g

DINNER
2 serving
20 minutes
20 minutes

Greek Chicken Skewers with Cauliflower Rice

Ingredients

- 1 pound boneless, skinless chicken breast, cut into bite-sized pieces
- 2 tbsp olive oil
- 2 tbsp lemon juice
- 2 cloves garlic, minced
- 1 tsp dried oregano
- 1 tsp dried thyme
- Salt and black pepper to taste
- Wooden or metal skewers

For the Tzatziki Sauce:
- 1 cup Greek yogurt
- 1/2 cucumber, grated and excess water squeezed out
- 1 clove garlic, minced
- 1 tbsp fresh dill, chopped (or 1 tsp dried dill)
- 1 tbsp lemon juice
- Salt and black pepper to taste

For the Cauliflower Rice:
- 1 medium head of cauliflower, grated or processed into rice-sized pieces
- 1 tbsp olive oil
- Salt and black pepper to taste

Instructions

1. In a bowl, mix olive oil, lemon juice, minced garlic, dried oregano, dried thyme, salt, and pepper.
2. Add the chicken pieces and toss to coat. Marinate for at least 30 minutes or up to 2 hours in the refrigerator.
3. Thread the marinated chicken onto skewers.
4. Preheat grill or grill pan to medium-high heat. Grill the skewers for 10-12 minutes, turning occasionally, until the chicken is cooked through and has nice grill marks.
5. In a bowl, combine Greek yogurt, grated cucumber, minced garlic, fresh dill, lemon juice, salt, and pepper.
6. Mix well and adjust seasoning to taste. Chill in the refrigerator until ready to serve.
7. Heat olive oil in a large skillet over medium heat.
8. Add the grated cauliflower and cook, stirring frequently, for about 5-7 minutes or until tender.
9. Season with salt and pepper to taste.
10. Serve the Greek chicken skewers on plates alongside the cauliflower rice.
11. Spoon the tzatziki sauce over the chicken or serve on the side for dipping.

Nutrition: Cal 420; Fat 22g; Carb 20g; Protein 40g

2 serving

50 minutes

15 minutes

DINNER

Spaghetti Squash with Fish Balls

Ingredients

For the Spaghetti Squash:
- 1 medium spaghetti squash
- 1 tbsp olive oil
- Salt and black pepper to taste

For the Fish Balls:
- 1/2 pound white fish fillets (like cod or haddock), finely chopped
- 1/4 cup breadcrumbs (gluten-free if needed)
- 1 egg
- 1 tbsp chopped fresh parsley
- 1 tsp garlic powder
- 1/2 tsp onion powder
- Salt and black pepper to taste
- 1 tbsp olive oil for cooking

For the Sauce (optional):
- 1/2 cup marinara sauce (store-bought or homemade, low-sugar)
- 1/4 cup grated Parmesan cheese (optional for garnish)

Instructions

1. Preheat your oven to 400°F (200°C).
2. Cut the spaghetti squash in half lengthwise and scoop out the seeds.
3. Brush the cut sides with olive oil and season with salt and pepper.
4. Place the squash cut-side down on a baking sheet lined with parchment paper.
5. Roast in the preheated oven for 40-50 minutes, or until the flesh reaches a state of tenderness and easily shredded with a fork.
6. In a mixing bowl, combine finely chopped fish, breadcrumbs, egg, parsley, garlic powder, onion powder, salt, and pepper. Mix until well combined.
7. Shape the mixture into small balls (about 1 inch in diameter).
8. Heat olive oil in a skillet over medium heat. Cook the fish balls for 4-5 minutes on each side, or until golden brown and cooked through.
9. Heat the marinara sauce in a small saucepan over low heat until warmed through.
10. Once the spaghetti squash is cooked, use a fork to scrape the flesh into strands.
11. Divide the spaghetti squash strands between serving plates.
12. Top with fish balls.
13. If using marinara sauce, drizzle it over the squash and fish balls.
14. Garnish with grated Parmesan cheese if desired.

Nutrition: Cal 350; Fat 18g; Carb 25g; Protein 25g

DINNER
2 serving
25 minutes
10 minutes

Baked Cod with Asparagus and Hollandaise Sauce

Ingredients

- 2 cod fillets (about 6 ounces each)
- 1 tbsp olive oil
- 1 tsp paprika
- 1/2 tsp garlic powder
- Salt and black pepper to taste
- Lemon wedges for serving

For the Asparagus:
- 1 bunch of asparagus, trimmed
- 1 tbsp olive oil
- Salt and black pepper to taste

For the Hollandaise Sauce:
- 2 large egg yolks
- 1/4 cup unsalted butter (1/2 stick), melted
- 1 tbsp lemon juice
- 1/2 tsp Dijon mustard
- Salt and white pepper to taste

Instructions

1. Preheat your oven to 400°F (200°C).
2. Place the cod fillets on a baking sheet lined with parchment paper or lightly greased.
3. Brush the fillets with olive oil. Sprinkle paprika, garlic powder, salt, and black pepper over the cod.
4. Bake in the preheated oven for 12–15 minutes, or until the cod flakes easily with a fork.
5. While the cod is baking, toss the trimmed asparagus with olive oil, salt, and black pepper.
6. Spread the asparagus on a separate baking sheet.
7. Roast in the oven (you can put it in with the cod if there is space) for about 10 minutes, or until tender and slightly crispy.
8. In a heatproof bowl (preferably a metal or glass bowl), whisk the egg yolks until they become thick and pale.
9. Place the bowl over a pot of simmering water (double boiler method) and continue whisking.
10. Slowly drizzle in the melted butter while whisking continuously until the sauce begins to thicken.
11. Remove from heat and whisk in lemon juice, Dijon mustard, salt, and white pepper.
12. Keep the sauce warm (but not hot) until ready to serve.
13. Arrange the baked cod fillets and roasted asparagus on plates.
14. Spoon the hollandaise sauce over the cod. Garnish with lemon wedges.

Nutrition: Cal 350; Fat 22g; Carb 9g; Protein 32g

2 serving

10 minutes

20 minutes

DINNER

Zucchini Noodles with Pesto and Shrimp

Ingredients

- 2 medium zucchinis, spiralized into noodles
- 1/2 pound shrimp, peeled and deveined
- 2 tbsp pesto sauce (store-bought or homemade)
- 1 tbsp olive oil
- 1 clove garlic, minced
- Salt and black pepper to taste
- Optional: Grated Parmesan cheese for garnish

Instructions

1. Spiralize the zucchinis to create noodles.
2. Peel and devein the shrimp.
3. Mince the garlic.
4. Heat 1 tbsp of olive oil in a large skillet over medium heat.
5. Add the minced garlic and cook for about 30 seconds, or until fragrant.
6. Add the shrimp to the skillet. Cook for 2-3 minutes per side, or until the shrimp turn pink and are cooked through. Season with salt and black pepper. Remove the shrimp from the skillet and set aside.
7. In the same skillet, add a little more olive oil if needed.
8. Add the spiralized zucchini noodles and cook for 2-3 minutes, or until they are tender but still slightly crisp. Avoid overcooking to prevent the noodles from becoming mushy.
9. Return the cooked shrimp to the skillet with the zucchini noodles.
10. Add the pesto sauce and toss everything together to coat the noodles and shrimp evenly. Cook for an additional 1-2 minutes to heat through.
11. Taste and adjust seasoning with additional salt and pepper if needed.
12. Garnish with grated Parmesan cheese if desired.
13. Divide the zucchini noodles and shrimp between two plates and serve hot.

Nutrition: Cal 290; Fat 15g; Carb 10g; Protein 28g

DINNER — 2 serving — 15 minutes — 10 minutes

Chicken and Vegetable Stir-Fry

Ingredients

- 1 chicken breast, sliced into thin strips
- 1 cup broccoli florets
- 1 red bell pepper, sliced
- 1 carrot, julienned
- 2 tbsp olive oil
- 2 tbsp low sodium soy sauce
- 1 clove garlic, minced
- Salt and black pepper to taste
- Optional: 1 tsp sesame seeds for garnish

Instructions

1. Slice the chicken breast into thin strips. Cut the broccoli into small florets. Slice the red bell pepper. Julienne the carrot.
2. Heat 1 tbsp of olive oil in a large skillet or wok over medium-high heat.
3. Add the chicken strips and cook for about 5-7 minutes, or until the chicken is cooked through and no longer pink in the center. Season with a pinch of salt and black pepper.
4. Remove the chicken from the skillet and set aside.
5. In the same skillet, add the remaining 1 tbsp of olive oil.
6. Add minced garlic and cook for 30 seconds, or until fragrant.
7. Add the broccoli, red bell pepper, and carrot to the skillet. Stir-fry for about 4-5 minutes, or until the vegetables are tender-crisp.
8. Return the cooked chicken to the skillet with the vegetables.
9. Drizzle with soy sauce and stir to coat everything evenly. Cook for an additional 1-2 minutes to heat through.
10. Taste and adjust seasoning with additional salt and pepper if needed.
11. Garnish with sesame seeds if desired.
12. Divide the stir-fry between two plates and serve hot.

Nutrition: Cal 280; Fat 16g; Carb 13g; Protein 22g

2 serving

10 minutes

15 minutes

DINNER

Grilled Salmon with Avocado Salsa

Ingredients

- 2 salmon fillets (about 6 ounces each)
- 1 tbsp olive oil
- 1 tsp garlic powder
- 1 tsp paprika
- 1/2 tsp dried oregano
- Salt and black pepper to taste
- Lemon wedges for serving

For the Avocado Salsa:
- 1 ripe avocado, diced
- 1/2 cup cherry tomatoes, diced
- 1/4 cup red onion, finely chopped
- 1 tbsp fresh cilantro, chopped
- 1 tbsp lime juice
- Salt and black pepper to taste

Instructions

1. Preheat the grill to medium-high heat.
2. Brush both sides of the salmon fillets with olive oil.
3. Season the fillets with garlic powder, paprika, dried oregano, salt, and black pepper.
4. Place the salmon on the grill, skin-side down. Grill for about 4-5 minutes per side, or until the salmon is cooked through and flakes easily with a fork. Cooking times may vary depending on the thickness of the fillets.
5. Prepare the Avocado Salsa:
6. In a medium bowl, combine diced avocado, cherry tomatoes, red onion, and chopped cilantro.
7. Drizzle with lime juice and season with salt and black pepper to taste.
8. Gently toss to mix, being careful not to mash the avocado.
9. Transfer the grilled salmon fillets to plates.
10. Top each fillet with a generous spoonful of avocado salsa. Serve with lemon wedges on the side.

Nutrition: Cal 400; Fat 28g; Carb 12g; Protein 32g

DINNER · 2 serving · 5 minutes · 15 minutes

Coconut Shrimp with Mango Salsa

Ingredients

- 12 Large shrimp, peeled and deveined
- 1 cup Coconut flakes
- 1 Egg, beaten
- Olive oil for frying
- 1 Ripe mango, diced
- 1/2 Red bell pepper, diced
- 1/4 Red onion, diced
- 2 tbsp Fresh cilantro, chopped
- 1 Lime, juiced
- Salt and pepper to taste

Instructions

1. Dip each shrimp into the beaten egg, then coat with coconut flakes.
2. Heat olive oil in a skillet over medium-high heat. Fry coconut shrimp until golden brown and crispy, about 2-3 minutes per side.
3. In a bowl, mix diced mango, red bell pepper, red onion, chopped cilantro, lime juice, salt, and pepper to make the mango salsa.
4. Serve coconut shrimp with mango salsa on the side.

Nutrition: Cal 250; Fat 15g; Carb 20g; Protein 10g

2 serving

10 minutes

15 minutes

DINNER

Scallop and Warm Spinach Salad

Ingredients

- 1 pound fresh scallops, patted dry
- 6 cups fresh spinach leaves, washed and dried
- 1 cup cherry tomatoes, halved
- 1/4 cup red onion, thinly sliced
- 2 cloves garlic, minced
- 2 tbsp olive oil
- 2 tbsp balsamic vinegar
- Salt and pepper to taste
- Fresh lemon wedges (for serving)

Instructions

1. Season the scallops with salt and pepper on both sides.
2. Heat 1 tbsp of olive oil in a large skillet over medium-high heat.
3. Add the scallops to the skillet and cook for 2-3 minutes on each side until they are golden brown and cooked through. Remove from the skillet and set aside.
4. In the same skillet, add the remaining tbsp of olive oil.
5. Add the minced garlic and sauté for 1-2 minutes until fragrant.
6. Add the cherry tomatoes and sliced red onion to the skillet. Cook for 2-3 minutes until slightly softened.
7. Add the fresh spinach leaves to the skillet and toss gently until wilted.
8. Divide the warm spinach mixture between two serving plates.
9. Arrange the cooked scallops on top of the spinach.
10. Drizzle balsamic vinegar over the salad.
11. Garnish with fresh lemon wedges.
12. Serve immediately while the salad is warm.

Nutrition: Cal 250; Fat 12g; Carb 15g; Protein 25g

DINNER
2 serving
15 minutes
10 minutes

Blackened Tofu with Sesame Broccoli Slaw

Ingredients

- 6 ounces extra-firm tofu, cubed
- Herbs and seasonings of choice
- 2 tbsp coconut oil
- 2 cups broccoli slaw
- 2 tbsp sesame seeds

Instructions

1. Place the tofu cubes in a medium bowl. Add the herbs and seasoning and rub to coat the cubes.

2. Place 1 tbsp of the coconut oil in a large skillet over high heat. When melted, add the tofu and sauté for 3 to 4 minutes on each side, until blackened. Transfer to a bowl, cover, and keep warm.

3. Wipe out the skillet and then add the remaining 1 tbsp coconut oil and place over medium-high heat. When the oil has melted, add the broccoli slaw and stir-fry until desired tenderness, about 2 minutes.

4. Spread the sautéed slaw on individual plates, then top with the blackened tofu. Sprinkle on the sesame seeds and serve.

Nutrition: Cal 200; Fat 15g; Carb 9g; Protein 10g

2 serving

30 minutes

10 minutes

DINNER

Stuffed Bell Peppers with Quinoa

Ingredients

- 2 large bell peppers (any color)
- 1/2 cup quinoa
- 1 cup vegetable broth
- 1/2 cup black beans, drained and rinsed
- 1/2 cup corn kernels (fresh or frozen)
- 1/4 cup diced tomatoes
- 1/4 cup diced onion
- 1 clove garlic, minced
- 1/2 tsp ground cumin
- 1/2 tsp chili powder
- Salt and pepper to taste
- 1/4 cup shredded cheddar cheese (optional)
- Fresh cilantro or parsley for garnish (optional)

Instructions

1. Preheat your oven to 375°F (190°C).
2. Cut the tops off the bell peppers and remove the seeds and membranes. Rinse them under cold water and set aside.
3. In a medium saucepan, combine the quinoa and vegetable broth. Bring to a boil, then reduce the heat to low, cover, and simmer for 15-20 minutes, or until the quinoa is cooked and the broth is absorbed.
4. In a skillet, heat a little oil over medium heat. Add the diced onion and minced garlic, and sauté until translucent and fragrant, about 2-3 minutes.
5. Add the black beans, corn kernels, diced tomatoes, ground cumin, chili powder, salt, and pepper to the skillet. Stir well and cook for another 3-4 minutes, until heated through.
6. Once the quinoa is cooked, fluff it with a fork and add it to the skillet with the bean and vegetable mixture. Stir everything together until well combined.
7. Stuff each bell pepper with the quinoa mixture, pressing down gently to pack it in. Place the stuffed peppers in a baking dish.
8. If using cheese, sprinkle it over the tops of the stuffed peppers.
9. Cover the baking dish with aluminum foil and bake in the preheated oven for 20-25 minutes or until the peppers are tender.
10. Remove the foil and bake for an additional 5 minutes to melt the cheese and allow the tops of the peppers to brown slightly.
11. Garnish with fresh cilantro or parsley if desired before serving.

Nutrition: Cal 260; Fat 4g; Carb 49g; Protein 10g

DINNER

2 serving

20 minutes

10 minutes

Cauliflower Steak with Tahini Dressing

Ingredients

For the Cauliflower Steaks:
- 1 small head cauliflower
- 2 tbsp olive oil
- Salt and black pepper, to taste
- 1/2 tsp garlic powder
- 1/2 tsp smoked paprika
- 1/2 tsp dried thyme

For the Tahini Dressing:
- 2 tbsp tahini
- 2 tbsp water
- 1 tbsp lemon juice
- 1 clove garlic, minced
- Salt, to taste
- Black pepper, to taste

For Serving:
- Fresh parsley, chopped (optional)
- Lemon wedges (optional)

Instructions

1. Preheat your oven to 425°F (220°C). Line a baking sheet with parchment paper.

2. Remove the leaves and trim the stem of the cauliflower, keeping the core intact. Slice the cauliflower into 1-inch thick steaks. You should get 2 steaks from a small cauliflower.

3. In a small bowl, mix together the olive oil, garlic powder, smoked paprika, dried thyme, salt, and black pepper.

4. Brush both sides of each cauliflower steak with the seasoned olive oil mixture.

5. Place the cauliflower steaks on the prepared baking sheet and roast in the preheated oven for 15-20 minutes, flipping halfway through, or until tender and golden brown.

6. While the cauliflower is roasting, prepare the tahini dressing. In a small bowl, whisk together the tahini, water, lemon juice, minced garlic, salt, and black pepper until smooth and creamy. Adjust the consistency with more water if needed.

7. Once the cauliflower steaks are done, transfer them to serving plates. Drizzle with the tahini dressing.

8. Garnish with chopped fresh parsley and serve with lemon wedges on the side, if desired.

Nutrition: Cal 190; Fat 16g; Carb 10g; Protein 15g

2 serving

20 minutes

10 minutes

DINNER

Roasted Beetroot with Herbs

Ingredients

- 3 medium beetroots, peeled and cut into wedges
- 2 tbsp olive oil
- 1 tsp dried rosemary (or 2 tsp fresh rosemary, chopped)
- 2 teaspoons of fresh thyme, chopped, or 1 teaspoon of dried thyme
- 1 clove garlic, minced
- Salt and pepper to taste
- Optional: 1 tbsp balsamic vinegar or lemon juice for added flavor

Instructions

1. Preheat your oven to 400°F (200°C).
2. Peel and cut the beetroots into wedges. The size of the wedges should be uniform for even cooking.
3. In a large bowl, toss the beetroot wedges with olive oil, rosemary, thyme, minced garlic, salt, and pepper until well-coated.
4. Spread the seasoned beetroot wedges in a single layer on a baking sheet. Ensure that they are not overcrowded to allow for even roasting.
5. Roast in the preheated oven for 30-35 minutes, or until the beetroots are tender and slightly caramelized. You can check for tenderness by piercing a wedge with a fork.
6. If desired, drizzle with balsamic vinegar or lemon juice immediately after roasting for an extra layer of flavor.
7. Transfer the roasted beetroot to a serving dish and enjoy warm.

Nutrition: Cal 190; Fat 16g; Carb 10g; Protein 15g

DINNER
2 serving
15 minutes
15 minutes

Butterfly Salmon Steak with Pesto Sauce

Ingredients

- 2 salmon steaks, about 6 ounces each
- Salt and black pepper, to taste
- 1 tbsp olive oil

For the Pesto Sauce:
- 1 cup fresh basil leaves
- 1/4 cup pine nuts (or walnuts)
- 1/4 cup grated Parmesan cheese (optional for strict Galveston Diet)
- 2 cloves garlic
- 1/4 cup olive oil
- Juice of 1/2 lemon

Instructions

1. In a food processor or blender, combine basil, pine nuts, Parmesan cheese (if using), and garlic.
2. Pulse until the mixture is finely chopped.
3. With the processor running, slowly add olive oil until the pesto is smooth and well combined.
4. Season with lemon juice, salt, and pepper. Adjust seasoning to taste.
5. Preheat your grill or oven to medium-high heat (about 375°F or 190°C).
6. Season the salmon steaks with salt and black pepper.
7. Brush the salmon steaks with olive oil.
8. Grill: Place the salmon steaks on the grill and cook for 4-5 minutes per side, or until the salmon is cooked through and flakes easily with a fork.
9. Oven: Place the salmon steaks on a baking sheet and bake for 12-15 minutes, or until the salmon is cooked through and flakes easily with a fork.
10. Transfer the cooked salmon steaks to serving plates.
11. Spoon the pesto sauce over the salmon steaks.
12. Garnish with extra basil leaves or a lemon wedge if desired.

Nutrition: Cal 360; Fat 26g; Carb 4g; Protein 30g

2 serving

DINNER

25 minutes

15 minutes

Mushroom Stroganoff with Creamy Garlic Cauliflower Rice

Ingredients

For the Stroganoff:
- 2 1/2 cups halved or quartered button mushrooms
- 3 garlic cloves, minced
- 1/2 medium yellow onion, thinly sliced
- 1 cup vegetable broth
- 2 tsp smoked paprika
- 1 tbsp plain full-fat Greek yogurt
- Salt and black pepper, to taste
- 2 tbsp chopped fresh parsley

For the Cauliflower Rice:
- 1/2 medium cauliflower, trimmed and cut into florets
- 1 1/2 tbsp olive oil
- 1 garlic clove, minced
- 3/4 tsp salt
- 1/2 tsp black pepper
- 1/4 cup vegetable broth
- 2 tbsp ghee (clarified butter) or unsalted butter
- 2 tbsp heavy cream

Instructions

For the Mushroom Stroganoff:
1. eat 1 tbsp of olive oil in a large skillet over medium heat. Add the mushrooms and cook until they release their moisture and start to brown, about 5-7 minutes. Remove the mushrooms from the skillet and set aside.
2. In the same skillet, add the remaining olive oil. Add the minced garlic and sliced onion. Sauté until the onion is soft and translucent, about 3-4 minutes.
3. Return the cooked mushrooms to the skillet. Stir in the vegetable broth and smoked paprika. Bring to a simmer and cook for 5-7 minutes, allowing the flavors to meld.
4. Reduce the heat to low. Stir in the Greek yogurt until well-combined and creamy. Season with salt and black pepper to taste.
5. Remove from heat and stir in chopped fresh parsley.

For the Creamy Garlic Cauliflower Rice:
1. In a food processor, pulse the cauliflower florets until they resemble rice grains.
2. Heat the olive oil in a large skillet over medium heat. Add the minced garlic and cook until fragrant, about 1 minute.
3. Add the riced cauliflower to the skillet. Season with salt and black pepper. Stir to combine.
4. Pour in the vegetable broth and cook until the cauliflower is tender and the broth has evaporated, about 5-7 minutes.
5. Add the ghee or unsalted butter and heavy cream to the cauliflower rice. Stir until the butter is melted and the cauliflower is creamy.
6. Divide the creamy garlic cauliflower rice among serving plates. Top with mushroom stroganoff. Garnish with additional chopped parsley if desired.

Nutrition: Cal 372; Fat 31g; Carb 17g; Protein 8g

SNACKS

2 serving

30 minutes

10 minutes

Coconut Matcha Energy Balls

Ingredients

- 1/2 cup shredded coconut
- 4 dates, pitted
- 1 tbsp matcha powder
- 1 tbsp coconut oil

Instructions

1. If the dates are dry, soak them in warm water for 10 minutes to soften. Drain and pat dry before using.

2. In a food processor, combine the shredded coconut, dates, matcha powder, and coconut oil. Process until the mixture is well-combined and starts to clump together. The mixture should be sticky and hold together when pressed.

3. Using your hands or a small cookie scoop, form the mixture into 8-10 balls. If the mixture is too sticky, you can lightly coat your hands with a bit of coconut oil.

4. Place the energy balls on a parchment-lined tray or plate and refrigerate for at least 30 minutes to set.

5. Serve the energy balls chilled or at room temperature. Store any leftovers in an airtight container in the refrigerator for up to a week.

Nutrition: Cal 80; Fat 5g; Carb 9g; Protein 1g

2 serving

SNACKS

15 minutes

10 minutes

Kale Chips

Ingredients

- 2 cups kale leaves, torn into bite-sized pieces
- 1 tbsp olive oil
- 1/4 tsp sea salt
- 1/4 tsp garlic powder

Instructions

1. Preheat your oven to 350°F (175°C). Line a baking sheet with parchment paper or a silicone baking mat.
2. Wash and thoroughly dry the kale leaves. Tear the leaves into bite-sized pieces, discarding any tough stems.
3. In a large bowl, toss the kale pieces with olive oil, sea salt, and garlic powder until evenly coated.
4. Spread the kale pieces in a single layer on the prepared baking sheet. Make sure the pieces are not overlapping to ensure they crisp up evenly.
5. Bake for 10-15 minutes, tossing halfway through, until the kale is crisp and lightly browned. Watch closely towards the end to prevent burning.
6. Allow the kale chips to cool on the baking sheet for a few minutes before serving. They will become even crisper as they cool.

Nutrition: Cal 80; Fat 7g; Carb 6g; Protein 2g

SNACKS

2 serving

10 minutes

10 minutes

Smoked Salmon Cucumber Bites

Ingredients

- 1/2 cucumber, sliced into 1/4-inch rounds
- 2 ounces smoked salmon
- 2 tbsp cream cheese
- 1 tsp capers
- Fresh dill for garnish

Instructions

1. Slice the cucumber into 1/4-inch thick rounds. Arrange the slices on a serving plate.
2. Spread a small amount of cream cheese on each cucumber slice.
3. Tear or cut the smoked salmon into bite-sized pieces and place a piece on top of each cucumber slice with cream cheese.
4. Top each bite with a caper and a small sprig of fresh dill.
5. Serve immediately or chill in the refrigerator until ready to serve.

Nutrition: Cal 150; Fat 10g; Carb 4g; Protein 12g

2 serving

12 minutes

10 minutes

SNACKS

Almond Flour Crackers with Guacamole

Ingredients

For the Crackers:
- 1/2 cup almond flour
- 1/4 tsp sea salt
- 1/4 tsp garlic powder
- 1/4 tsp dried rosemary
- 1 tbsp olive oil
- 1 tbsp water

For the Guacamole:
- 1 avocado, mashed
- 1 tbsp lime juice
- 1 tbsp chopped cilantro
- Salt to taste (optional)

Instructions

1. Preheat your oven to 350°F (175°C).

2. In a bowl, combine almond flour, sea salt, garlic powder, and dried rosemary.

3. Add olive oil and water, mixing until a dough forms.

4. Place the dough between two sheets of parchment paper. Roll it out to about 1/8-inch thickness.

5. Remove the top sheet of parchment paper. Use a knife or pizza cutter to cut the dough into small squares or rectangles.

6. Transfer the parchment paper with the cut dough onto a baking sheet.

7. Bake for 10-12 minutes or until the edges are golden brown. Keep an eye on them to avoid burning.

8. Let the crackers cool completely on the baking sheet before breaking them apart.

9. In a bowl, mash the avocado with a fork. Stir in lime juice and chopped cilantro. Season with salt if desired.

10. Serve the almond flour crackers with a generous side of guacamole.

Nutrition: Cal 250; Fat 21g; Carb 10g; Protein 6g

SNACKS

2 serving

30 minutes

10 minutes

Baba Ganoush

Ingredients

- 2 medium eggplants
- 2 cloves garlic, minced
- 2 tbsp tahini
- 2 tbsp lemon juice
- 1 tbsp extra-virgin olive oil
- 1/4 tsp ground cumin
- Salt and pepper to taste
- Chopped fresh parsley for garnish

Instructions

1. Preheat your oven to 400°F (200°C).
2. Prick the eggplants all over with a fork. Place them on a baking sheet lined with parchment paper.
3. Roast the eggplants in the preheated oven for about 25-30 minutes, or until they are very soft and the skin is charred.
4. Remove the eggplants from the oven and let them cool slightly.
5. Once cool enough to handle, slice the eggplants in half lengthwise and scoop out the flesh into a bowl. Discard the charred skin.
6. Add minced garlic, tahini, lemon juice, olive oil, ground cumin, salt, and pepper to the bowl with the eggplant flesh.
7. Use a fork or potato masher to mash the mixture until smooth. Alternatively, you can use a food processor for a smoother texture.
8. Taste the baba ganoush and adjust the seasoning if needed, adding more salt, lemon juice, or tahini to your preference.
9. Transfer the baba ganoush to a serving dish, drizzle with a little extra olive oil, and garnish with chopped fresh parsley.
10. Serve the baba ganoush with Galveston Diet-approved veggie sticks, flaxseed crackers, or use it as a spread on sandwiches or wraps.

Nutrition: Cal 90; Fat 6g; Carb 10g; Protein 2g

2 serving

0 minutes

10 minutes

SNACKS

Herbed White Bean Dip

Ingredients

- 1 cup cooked cannellini beans
- 1 lemon, juiced (about 3 tbsps)
- 2 tsp grated lemon zest
- 4 tbsp tahini or soy sauce
- 2 tbsp olive oil
- 2 tbsp chopped fresh dill
- 2 garlic cloves

Instructions

1. In a food processor, combine the cooked cannellini beans, lemon juice, lemon zest, tahini or soy sauce, olive oil, chopped fresh dill, and garlic cloves.

2. Blend the mixture until smooth and creamy, scraping down the sides of the food processor as needed.

3. Taste the white bean dip and adjust seasoning if necessary, adding salt and pepper to taste.

4. Transfer the herbed white bean dip to a serving bowl.

5. Serve immediately with Galveston Diet-approved veggie sticks, flaxseed crackers, or use it as a spread on sandwiches or wraps.

Nutrition: Cal 230; Fat 16g; Carb 18g; Protein 7g

Mushroom Caviar Dip

Ingredients

- 2 cups mushrooms, finely chopped
- 1 onion, finely chopped
- 2 garlic cloves, minced
- 2 tbsp olive oil
- 1 tbsp balsamic vinegar
- 1 tbsp coconut aminos (a soy sauce alternative)
- 1 tsp smoked paprika
- Salt and pepper to taste
- Chopped fresh parsley for garnish

Instructions

1. Heat olive oil in a skillet over medium heat. Add chopped onions and garlic, and sauté until onions are translucent and fragrant, about 3-4 minutes.

2. Add finely chopped mushrooms to the skillet and cook until they release their moisture and start to brown, stirring occasionally, about 8-10 minutes.

3. Once mushrooms are cooked, stir in balsamic vinegar, coconut aminos, smoked paprika, salt, and pepper. Cook for another 2-3 minutes to allow flavors to meld.

4. Remove from heat and let the mixture cool slightly.

5. Transfer the mushroom mixture to a food processor and pulse a few times until you reach the desired consistency. You can make it smooth or leave it slightly chunky, depending on your preference.

6. Transfer the mushroom caviar dip to a serving bowl and garnish with chopped fresh parsley.

7. Serve warm or at room temperature with your favorite Galveston Diet-approved crackers, bread, or vegetable sticks.

Nutrition: Cal 80; Fat 5g; Carb 7g; Protein 3g

2 serving

10 minutes

10 minutes

SNACKS

Deviled Eggs

Ingredients

- 4 hard-boiled large eggs
- 2 tbsp avocado oil mayonnaise
- 2 tbsp chia seeds
- ½ tsp ground turmeric
- ½ green bell pepper, cored and sliced

Instructions

1. Peel the hard-boiled eggs, cut each in half lengthwise, and gently remove the yolks. Place the egg whites on a serving plate.

2. In a small bowl, mash the egg yolks with a fork. Add the avocado oil mayonnaise, chia seeds, and ground turmeric to the mashed yolks. Mix until well combined and smooth.

3. Using a spoon or a piping bag, evenly distribute the yolk mixture into the hollows of the egg whites.

4. Arrange the stuffed eggs on the serving plate.

5. Serve the deviled eggs with the strips of green bell pepper on the side.

Nutrition: Cal   200;   Fat   14g;   Carb   8g;   Protein   10g

SNACKS

2 serving

15 minutes

10 minutes

Prosciutto-Wrapped Asparagus

Ingredients

- 6 asparagus spears, trimmed
- 3 slices prosciutto, halved lengthwise
- 1 tbsp olive oil
- Salt and pepper to taste

Instructions

1. Preheat your oven to 400°F (200°C).
2. Wrap each asparagus spear with a half slice of prosciutto, starting at the bottom and spiraling up to the tip.
3. Place the wrapped asparagus on a baking sheet. Drizzle with olive oil and season with salt and pepper.
4. Bake in the preheated oven for 10-15 minutes, or until the prosciutto is crispy and the asparagus is tender.
5. Remove from the oven and serve warm.

Nutrition: Cal   180;   Fat   13g;   Carb   3g;   Protein   12g

2 serving

0 minutes

15 minutes

SNACKS

Mango Salsa with Jicama Chips

Ingredients

- 1 ripe mango, diced
- 1/4 red onion, finely chopped
- 1/4 red bell pepper, diced
- 1 tbsp lime juice
- 1 tbsp chopped cilantro
- 1 small jicama, peeled and sliced into chips

Instructions

1. In a mixing bowl, combine the diced mango, finely chopped red onion, and diced red bell pepper.
2. Add lime juice and chopped cilantro. Mix well to combine.
3. Taste and adjust seasoning as needed (you may add a pinch of salt or extra lime juice if desired).
4. Refrigerate the salsa until ready to serve.
5. Peel the jicama and slice it into thin chips.
6. If desired, you can lightly season the chips with a pinch of sea salt or other spices.
7. Arrange the jicama chips on a serving plate.
8. Spoon the mango salsa into a serving bowl and place it alongside the jicama chipS.

Nutrition: Cal 120; Fat 0g; Carb 30g; Protein 2g

SNACKS

2 serving

0 minutes

15 minutes

Edamame Hummus

Ingredients

- 1 cup shelled edamame, cooked
- 1/4 cup tahini
- 2 tbsp lemon juice
- 1 clove garlic, minced
- 1/4 tsp sea salt
- 2 tbsp olive oil
- Water to thin, if needed

Instructions

1. In a food processor, combine the cooked edamame, tahini, lemon juice, minced garlic, sea salt, and olive oil.

2. Blend the mixture until smooth and creamy. If the hummus is too thick, gradually add water, a tbsp at a time until the desired consistency is reached.

3. Taste and adjust seasoning if necessary, adding more salt or lemon juice as desired.

4. Transfer the hummus to a serving bowl. Garnish with a drizzle of olive oil or additional sea salt if desired.

5. Store leftovers in an airtight container in the refrigerator for up to 5 days.

Nutrition: Cal   130;   Fat   9g;   Carb   10g;   Protein   5g

2 serving

0 minutes

15 minutes

SNACKS

Stuffed Dates with Almonds and Goat Cheese

Ingredients

- 12 Medjool dates, pitted
- 12 almonds
- 1/4 cup goat cheese, softened
- 1 tbsp honey (optional, for drizzling)
- Fresh rosemary or thyme for garnish (optional)

Instructions

1. Using a small knife, carefully slice each date lengthwise on one side to create an opening, but do not cut all the way through. Remove the pit if it's not already removed.

2. Stuff each date with an almond and a small spoonful of goat cheese. Press the date closed to secure the stuffing.

3. Drizzle with honey if desired for added sweetness.

4. Garnish with a small sprig of fresh rosemary or thyme for a touch of elegance.

5. Arrange the stuffed dates on a serving platter.

Nutrition: Cal 120; Fat 8g; Carb 12g; Protein 3g

SNACKS

2 serving

25 minutes

10 minutes

Eggplant Chips with Tahini Dip

Ingredients

For the Eggplant Chips:
- 1 medium eggplant, sliced thinly
- 1 tbsp olive oil
- 1/4 tsp sea salt

For the Tahini Dip:
- 1/4 cup tahini
- 1 tbsp lemon juice
- 1 clove garlic, minced
- Water to thin dip as needed

Instructions

1. Preheat your oven to 400°F (200°C). Line a baking sheet with parchment paper.

2. Arrange the eggplant slices in a single layer on the baking sheet. Brush each slice lightly with olive oil and sprinkle with sea salt.

3. Bake for 20-25 minutes, flipping halfway through, until the eggplant chips are crispy and golden brown. Keep an eye on them to avoid burning.

4. In a small bowl, whisk together tahini, lemon juice, and minced garlic. The mixture will be thick.

5. Gradually add water, a tbsp at a time, until the dip reaches your desired consistency. It should be smooth and creamy but not too runny.

6. Once the eggplant chips are baked and cooled slightly, serve them with the tahini dip on the side.

Nutrition: Cal 120; Fat 9g; Carb 8g; Protein 4g

2 serving

10 minutes

10 minutes

SNACKS

Zucchini Fritters

Ingredients

- 1 medium zucchini, grated
- 1 egg, beaten
- 1/4 cup almond flour
- 1/4 tsp garlic powder
- Salt and pepper to taste
- 1 tbsp olive oil (for frying)

Instructions

1. Grate the zucchini and place it in a clean kitchen towel or cheesecloth. Squeeze out excess moisture by twisting the towel to remove as much liquid as possible. This step is crucial for crispy fritters.

2. In a medium bowl, combine the grated zucchini, beaten egg, almond flour, garlic powder, salt, and pepper. Mix well until all ingredients are thoroughly combined.

3. Heat olive oil in a non-stick skillet over medium heat. Scoop 2-3 tbsps of the zucchini mixture per fritter and flatten it slightly with the back of a spoon or spatula.

4. Cook the fritters in the skillet for about 3-4 minutes on each side, or until they are golden brown and crispy. Flip carefully to avoid breaking.

5. Remove the fritters from the skillet and place them on a paper towel-lined plate to drain any excess oil. Serve warm.

Nutrition: Cal 80; Fat 6 g; Carb 4g; Protein 3g

SNACKS

2 serving

30 minutes

15 minutes

Walnut Cocoa Balls

Ingredients

- 1 cup walnuts
- 1/4 cup cocoa powder
- 1/4 cup collagen powder (unflavored or chocolate-flavored)
- 1/4 cup almond butter or cashew butter
- 2 tbsp honey or maple syrup
- 1 tsp vanilla extract
- Pinch of sea salt

Instructions

1. Place the walnuts in a food processor and pulse until they are finely ground but not turned into a paste.
2. Add the cocoa powder, collagen powder, almond butter, honey or maple syrup, vanilla extract, and a pinch of sea salt to the food processor with the ground walnuts.
3. Process until the mixture is well combined and starts to come together. It should be slightly sticky and hold together when pressed.
4. Using your hands, scoop out small portions of the mixture and roll them into bite-sized balls (about 1 inch in diameter).
5. Place the balls on a plate or baking sheet lined with parchment paper.
6. Refrigerate the balls for at least 30 minutes to firm up.
7. Enjoy the walnut cocoa collagen balls as a snack or a post-workout treat. Store leftovers in an airtight container in the refrigerator for up to 2 weeks.

Nutrition: Cal   90;   Fat   7g;   Carb   6g;   Protein   3g

2 serving

15 minutes

15 minutes

DESSERTS

Pumpkin Oatmeal Cookies

Ingredients

- 1/2 cup canned pumpkin puree
- 2 tbsp honey or maple syrup
- 2 tbsp coconut oil, melted
- 1/2 egg (whisk an egg and use half of it)
- 1/2 tsp vanilla extract
- 3/4 cup rolled oats
- 1/2 cup whole wheat flour
- 1/2 tsp baking powder
- 1/4 tsp cinnamon
- Pinch of nutmeg
- Pinch of salt

Instructions

1. Preheat oven to 350°F (175°C) and line a baking sheet with parchment paper.
2. In a large bowl, mix pumpkin puree, honey or maple syrup, melted coconut oil, half of an egg, and vanilla extract.
3. Add rolled oats, whole wheat flour, baking powder, cinnamon, nutmeg, and salt. Stir until well combined.
4. Drop spoonfuls of dough onto the prepared baking sheet and flatten slightly with the back of a spoon.
5. Bake for 12-15 minutes or until edges are golden brown.
6. Allow to cool on the baking sheet for 5 minutes before transferring to a wire rack to cool completely.

Nutrition: Cal   220;   Fat   10g;   Carb   30g;   Protein   5g

DESSERTS

2 serving

25 minutes

15 minutes

Zucchini Carrot Muffins

Ingredients

- 1/2 cup grated zucchini
- 1/2 cup grated carrots
- 2 tbsp honey or maple syrup
- 2 tbsp unsweetened applesauce
- 1 egg
- 1/2 tsp vanilla extract
- 1/2 cup whole wheat flour
- 1/4 cup almond flour
- 1/2 tsp baking powder
- 1/4 tsp baking soda
- 1/2 tsp cinnamon
- Pinch of salt

Instructions

1. Preheat oven to 350°F (175°C) and line a muffin tin with paper liners.
2. In a large bowl, mix grated zucchini, grated carrots, honey or maple syrup, applesauce, egg, and vanilla extract.
3. Add whole wheat flour, almond flour, baking powder, baking soda, cinnamon, and salt. Stir until just combined.
4. Divide the batter evenly among the muffin cups.
5. Bake for 20-25 minutes or until a toothpick inserted into the center comes out clean.
6. Allow to cool in the pan for 5 minutes before transferring to a wire rack to cool completely.

Nutrition: Cal 200; Fat 5g; Carb 30g; Protein 6g

2 serving

25 minutes

15 minutes

DESSERTS

Avocado Chocolate Brownies

Ingredients

- 1/2 ripe avocado, mashed
- 2 tbsp honey or maple syrup
- 2 tbsp unsweetened applesauce
- 2 tbsp cocoa powder
- 2 tbsp almond flour
- 1 egg
- 1/2 tsp vanilla extract
- 1/4 tsp baking powder
- Pinch of salt

Instructions

1. Preheat the oven to 350°F (175°C) and grease a small baking dish.
2. In a mixing bowl, combine mashed avocado, honey or maple syrup, and applesauce.
3. Add cocoa powder, almond flour, egg, vanilla extract, baking powder, and salt. Mix until well combined.
4. Pour the batter into the prepared baking dish and smooth the top.
5. Bake for 20-25 minutes or until a toothpick inserted into the center comes out clean.
6. Allow to cool before slicing into squares.

Nutrition: Cal 180; Fat 12g; Carb 20g; Protein 4g

DESSERTS

2 serving

5 minutes

10 minutes

Grilled Pineapple with Coconut Whipped Cream

Ingredients

- 4 pineapple slices
- 1/2 cup canned coconut milk (full-fat), refrigerated overnight
- 1/2 tsp vanilla extract
- 1 tbsp unsweetened shredded coconut (optional)

Instructions

1. Preheat the grill to medium-high heat.
2. Grill pineapple slices for 2-3 minutes on each side or until caramelized grill marks form.
3. While the pineapple is grilling, make the coconut whipped cream. Scoop out the solid coconut cream from the chilled coconut milk can (discard the liquid) and place it in a mixing bowl. Add vanilla extract and whip until fluffy.
4. Serve the grilled pineapple slices with a dollop of coconut whipped cream on top.
5. Optional: sprinkle with unsweetened shredded coconut for extra flavor and texture.

Nutrition: Cal 150; Fat 12g; Carb 10g; Protein 1g

2 serving

0 minutes

10 minutes

DESSERTS

Chocolate Avocado Mousse

Ingredients

- 1 ripe avocado
- 2 tbsp unsweetened cocoa powder
- 2 tbsp coconut milk (or almond milk)
- 1-2 tbsp honey or maple syrup (optional)
- 1/2 tsp vanilla extract
- Pinch of salt
- Fresh berries for garnish (optional)

Instructions

1. Scoop the flesh of the avocado into a blender or food processor.
2. Add cocoa powder, coconut milk, honey or maple syrup (if using), vanilla extract, and a pinch of salt.
3. Blend until smooth and creamy.
4. Taste and adjust sweetness if necessary by adding more honey or maple syrup.
5. Transfer the mousse to two serving dishes.
6. Chill in the refrigerator for at least 30 minutes before serving.
7. Garnish with fresh berries if desired.

Nutrition: Cal 150; Fat 10g; Carb 15g; Protein 2g

DESSERTS

2 serving

2 hours

10 minutes

Chia Seed Pudding with Mango

Ingredients

- 1/4 cup chia seeds
- 1 cup coconut milk
- 1 tsp vanilla extract
- 1 tbsp maple syrup (optional, for sweetness)
- 1/2 cup diced mango

Instructions

1. In a medium bowl, combine chia seeds, coconut milk, vanilla extract, and maple syrup (if using).

2. Stir well to ensure the chia seeds are evenly distributed and not clumping together.

3. Cover the bowl with a lid or plastic wrap and refrigerate for at least 2 hours or overnight. This allows the chia seeds to absorb the liquid and expand, creating a pudding-like texture.

4. While the chia pudding is setting, dice the mango into small pieces.

5. After the chia pudding has set, stir it well to break up any clumps.

6. Spoon the pudding into serving bowls or glasses. Top with diced mango.

7. Garnish with additional fresh mango, a sprinkle of coconut flakes, or a few mint leaves if desired.

Nutrition: Cal 230; Fat 15g; Carb 20g; Protein 4g

2 serving

2 hours

10 minutes

DESSERTS

Pumpkin Pie Chia Pudding

Ingredients

- 1/4 cup chia seeds
- 1 cup almond milk
- 1/4 cup pumpkin puree
- 1/2 tsp pumpkin pie spice
- 1 tbsp maple syrup (optional)

Instructions

1. In a medium bowl, mix together 1/4 cup chia seeds, 1 cup almond milk, 1/4 cup pumpkin puree, 1/2 tsp pumpkin pie spice, and 1 tbsp maple syrup (if using).
2. Stir well to ensure the chia seeds are evenly distributed and all ingredients are combined.
3. Cover the bowl with a lid or plastic wrap.
4. Refrigerate for at least 2 hours or overnight. The chia seeds will absorb the liquid and create a pudding-like consistency.
5. Once the chia pudding has set, stir it to break up any clumps.
6. Divide the pudding evenly between 2 serving bowls or glasses.
7. Garnish with a sprinkle of additional pumpkin pie spice, a dollop of whipped coconut cream, or some toasted pecans if desired.

Nutrition: Cal 200; Fat 10g; Carb 22g; Protein 5g

DESSERTS

2 serving

15 minutes

10 minutes

Coconut Macaroons

Ingredients

- 1 cup shredded coconut
- 2 egg whites
- 1 tbsp honey
- 1/4 tsp vanilla extract

Instructions

1. Preheat your oven to 325°F (163°C).
2. Line a baking sheet with parchment paper or a silicone baking mat.
3. In a medium bowl, whisk the 2 egg whites until they form soft peaks.
4. Gently fold in 1 cup shredded coconut, 1 tbsp honey, and 1/4 tsp vanilla extract until evenly combined.
5. Using a spoon or cookie scoop, drop small mounds of the mixture onto the prepared baking sheet, spacing them about 1 inch apart.
6. Bake in the preheated oven for 10-12 minutes, or until the edges are golden brown and the macaroons are set.
7. Allow the macaroons to cool on the baking sheet for a few minutes before transferring them to a wire rack to cool completely.

Nutrition: Cal   80;   Fat   7g;   Carb   6g;   Protein   2g

2 serving

4 hours

10 minutes

DESSERTS

Coconut Milk Panna Cotta with Raspberry Sauce

Ingredients

- 1 cup coconut milk
- 1 tbsp honey
- 1/2 tsp vanilla extract
- 1 tsp gelatin

For the Raspberry Sauce:
- 1/4 cup raspberries
- 1 tbsp water

Instructions

1. In a small bowl, mix 1 tsp gelatin with 1 tbsp of water. Allow it to rest for 5 minutes to fully develop its flavors.

2. In a saucepan, combine 1 cup coconut milk and 1 tbsp honey. Heat over medium heat until the mixture is warm but not boiling.

3. Remove from heat and stir in the bloomed gelatin until fully dissolved.

4. Stir in 1/2 tsp vanilla extract.

5. Pour the coconut milk mixture into serving glasses or ramekins.

6. Refrigerate for at least 4 hours or until the panna cotta is set.

7. In a small saucepan, combine 1/4 cup raspberries and 1 tbsp water.

8. Heat over medium heat until the raspberries break down and the mixture thickens, about 5 minutes.

9. Use a spoon or a blender to smooth out the sauce if desired. Strain through a fine-mesh sieve if you prefer a smoother texture.

10. Once the panna cotta is set, spoon the raspberry sauce over the top before serving.

Nutrition: Cal 200; Fat 16g; Carb 15g; Protein 1g

DESSERTS

2 serving

30 minutes

10 minutes

Blueberry Almond Crumble

Ingredients

- 1 cup fresh or frozen blueberries
- 1/4 cup almond flour
- 1/4 cup chopped almonds
- 2 tbsp coconut oil
- 1 tbsp honey
- 1/2 tsp cinnamon

Instructions

1. Preheat your oven to 350°F (175°C).

2. If using frozen blueberries, thaw them slightly. Place the blueberries in a mixing bowl and set aside.

3. In a separate bowl, combine the almond flour, chopped almonds, coconut oil, honey, and cinnamon. Mix until the mixture resembles coarse crumbs.

4. Spread the blueberries evenly in a small baking dish or individual ramekins.

5. Sprinkle the crumble topping evenly over the blueberries.

6. Bake in the preheated oven for 25-30 minutes, or until the topping is golden brown and the blueberries are bubbling.

7. Allow the crumble to cool slightly before serving. Enjoy warm or at room temperature.

Nutrition: Cal 240; Fat 17g; Carb 19g; Protein 5g

2 serving

25 minutes

15 minutes

DESSERTS

Galveston Diet Texas Sheet Cake

Ingredients

For the Cake:
- 1 cup almond flour
- 1/2 cup coconut flour
- 1/2 cup unsweetened cocoa powder
- 1 tsp baking powder
- 1/2 tsp baking soda
- 1/4 tsp salt
- 1/2 cup erythritol or another low-carb sweetener
- 1/2 cup unsalted butter, melted
- 2 large eggs
- 1/2 cup unsweetened almond milk
- 1 tsp vanilla extract

For the Frosting:
- 1/2 cup unsalted butter
- 2 tbsp unsweetened cocoa powder
- 1/4 cup erythritol or another low-carb sweetener
- 2 tbsp unsweetened almond milk
- 1/2 tsp vanilla extract

Instructions

1. Preheat your oven to 350°F (175°C). Grease and line a 9x13 inch baking pan with parchment paper.
2. In a large bowl, whisk together almond flour, coconut flour, cocoa powder, baking powder, baking soda, salt, and erythritol.
3. In another bowl, mix melted butter, eggs, almond milk, and vanilla extract.
4. Combine the wet and dry ingredients and mix until smooth.
5. Pour the batter into the prepared baking pan and spread it evenly.
6. Bake in the preheated oven for 20-25 minutes, or until a toothpick inserted into the center comes out clean.
7. Allow the cake to cool completely in the pan on a wire rack before frosting.
8. In a medium saucepan over low heat, melt the butter.
9. Whisk in cocoa powder until smooth.
10. Remove from heat and whisk in erythritol, almond milk, and vanilla extract until well-combined and smooth.
11. Allow the frosting to slightly cool until it thickens to a spreadable consistency.
12. Spread the frosting evenly over the cooled cake.
13. Cut into squares and serve. Store any leftovers in an airtight container.

Nutrition: Cal 180; Fat 15g; Carb 8g; Protein 5g

DESSERTS

2 serving

2 hours

10 minutes

Yogurt Berry Ice Cream

Ingredients

- 2 cups plain Greek yogurt (full-fat or 2%)
- 1 cup mixed berries (such as strawberries, blueberries, raspberries), fresh or frozen
- 2 tbsp erythritol or another low-carb sweetener (adjust to taste)
- 1 tsp vanilla extract
- Juice of 1/2 lemon (optional, for a tangy flavor)

Instructions

1. If using fresh berries, wash and dry them. If using frozen berries, thaw them slightly to make blending easier.

2. In a blender or food processor, combine the berries, Greek yogurt, erythritol, vanilla extract, and lemon juice (if using).

3. Blend until smooth and creamy. Taste and adjust sweetness if needed by adding more erythritol.

4. Transfer the mixture to a bowl or a container and refrigerate for about 1-2 hours. This step is optional but helps the mixture firm up a bit before freezing.

5. Pour the chilled mixture into an ice cream maker and churn according to the manufacturer's instructions until it reaches a soft-serve consistency.

6. If you don't have an ice cream maker, pour the mixture into a freezer-safe container and freeze. At intervals of 30 minutes, forcefully agitate the mixture using a fork to break up ice crystals until it's firm and creamy, about 2-3 hours.

7. Scoop the ice cream into bowls or cones and serve immediately. If it's too hard after freezing, let it sit at room temperature for a few minutes to soften slightly before serving.

8. Store any leftovers in an airtight container in the freezer.

Nutrition: Cal 130; Fat 7g; Carb 10g; Protein 9g

2 serving
15 minutes
10 minutes

DESSERTS

Chocolate-Cinnamon Apple Bites

Ingredients

- 2 medium apples (such as Fuji or Gala), cored and sliced
- 2 tbsp almond butter or peanut butter
- 2 tbsp unsweetened cocoa powder
- 1 tbsp coconut oil
- 1 tbsp honey or maple syrup (optional, for added sweetness)
- 1/2 tsp ground cinnamon
- Pinch of sea salt

Instructions

1. Core the apples and slice them into thin rounds or wedges. You can leave the skin on for extra fiber or peel them if you prefer.
2. In a small saucepan, melt the coconut oil over low heat.
3. Once melted, stir in the cocoa powder until smooth. Add honey or maple syrup if using, and mix well.
4. Remove from heat and stir in the ground cinnamon and a pinch of sea salt.
5. Dip each apple slice into the chocolate mixture, making sure it is evenly coated.
6. Place the coated apple slices on a baking sheet lined with parchment paper.
7. Refrigerate the apple slices for about 10-15 minutes to allow the chocolate coating to firm up.
8. Serve the chocolate-cinnamon apple bites immediately or store them in an airtight container in the refrigerator for up to 3 days.

Nutrition: Cal   130;   Fat   10g;   Carb   10g;   Protein   2g

DESSERTS

2 serving

35 minutes

10 minutes

Blueberry Peach Cobbler

Ingredients

For the Filling:
- 2 cups fresh or frozen blueberries
- 2 cups fresh peaches, peeled and sliced (or frozen peaches, thawed)
- 2 tbsp honey or maple syrup (optional, for added sweetness)
- 1 tbsp lemon juice
- 1 tbsp arrowroot powder or cornstarch (to thicken)
- 1/2 tsp cinnamon
- 1/4 tsp nutmeg

For the Topping:
- 1/2 cup almond flour
- 1/4 cup coconut flour
- 1/4 cup chopped pecans or walnuts
- 2 tbsp coconut oil or unsalted butter, melted
- 2 tbsp honey or maple syrup
- 1/2 tsp vanilla extract
- 1/4 tsp sea salt

Instructions

1. Preheat your oven to 350°F (175°C).
2. In a large mixing bowl, combine blueberries, peach slices, honey or maple syrup (if using), lemon juice, arrowroot powder, cinnamon, and nutmeg. Toss well to coat.
3. Transfer the fruit mixture into a baking dish (about 8x8 inches or similar).
4. In a separate bowl, mix together almond flour, coconut flour, chopped pecans, melted coconut oil or butter, honey or maple syrup, vanilla extract, and sea salt.
5. Stir until the mixture resembles coarse crumbs.
6. Evenly sprinkle the topping mixture over the fruit filling.
7. Bake in the preheated oven for 30-35 minutes, or until the topping is golden brown and the fruit filling is bubbling.
8. Allow the cobbler to cool for about 10 minutes before serving. This will help the filling thicken up a bit more.

Nutrition: Cal 200; Fat 16g; Carb 16g; Protein 4g

2 serving

30 minutes

15 minutes

DESSERTS

Lemon Ricotta Berry Parfait

Ingredients

For the Ricotta Mixture:
- 1 cup ricotta cheese
- 1/2 cup plain Greek yogurt
- 2 tbsp honey or maple syrup (optional)
- Zest of 1 lemon
- 1 tbsp fresh lemon juice
- 1/2 tsp vanilla extract

For the Berry Layer:
- 1 cup fresh berries (such as strawberries, blueberries, raspberries, or a mix)
- 1 tbsp honey or maple syrup (optional, depending on berry sweetness)

Instructions

1. In a bowl, combine the ricotta cheese, Greek yogurt, honey or maple syrup (if using), lemon zest, lemon juice, and vanilla extract.

2. Mix until smooth and well combined. Adjust sweetness to taste if needed.

3. If using fresh berries, rinse and slice them as needed. If you prefer, you can lightly sweeten the berries with honey or maple syrup, depending on their natural sweetness.

4. In serving glasses or bowls, start by adding a layer of the lemon ricotta mixture.

5. Add a layer of berries on top of the ricotta.

6. Repeat the layers until the glasses are filled, finishing with a layer of berries on top.

7. Chill the parfaits in the refrigerator for at least 30 minutes before serving to let the flavors meld together

Nutrition: Cal 250; Fat 12g; Carb 20g; Protein 13g

28-Day Meal Plan

Day 1
- **Breakfast:** Tropical Mango Coconut Smoothie
- **Lunch:** Almond Chicken with Broccoli
- **Dinner:** Salmon and Asparagus Foil Packets

Day 2
- **Breakfast:** Chocolate Strawberry Smoothie
- **Lunch:** Stuffed Bell Peppers with Ground Beef and Quinoa
- **Dinner:** Baked Chicken with Brussels Sprouts

Day 3
- **Breakfast:** Mint Chocolate Chip Smoothie
- **Lunch:** Zoodles with Pesto Sauce and Turkey
- **Dinner:** Stuffed Zucchini Boats

Day 4
- **Breakfast:** Turmeric Ginger Detox Smoothie
- **Lunch:** Mushroom Cream Soup
- **Dinner:** Greek Chicken Skewers with Cauliflower Rice

Day 5
- **Breakfast:** Peanut Butter Banana Smoothie
- **Lunch:** Vegetable and Nut Stew
- **Dinner:** Spaghetti Squash with Fish Balls

Day 6
- **Breakfast:** Quinoa Breakfast Bowl
- **Lunch:** Mediterranean Chickpea Salad
- **Dinner:** Baked Cod with Asparagus and Hollandaise Sauce

Day 7
- **Breakfast:** Greek Yogurt Bowl
- **Lunch:** Quinoa and Black Bean Salad
- **Dinner:** Zucchini Noo-dles with Pesto and Shrimp

Day 8
- **Breakfast:** Flaxseed Meal Pancakes with Berries
- **Lunch:** Shrimp Avocado Salad
- **Dinner:** Chicken and Vegetable Stir-Fry

Day 9
- **Breakfast:** Oatmeal with Fresh Berries
- **Lunch:** Tuna and White Bean Salad
- **Dinner:** Grilled Salmon with Avocado Salsa

Day 10
- **Breakfast:** Spinach Omelette
- **Lunch:** Avocado and Turkey Wrap
- **Dinner:** Coconut Shrimp with Mango Salsa

Day 11
- **Breakfast:** Oat and Berry Acai Bowl
- **Lunch:** Cheeseburger Lettuce Sliders
- **Dinner:** Scallop and Warm Spinach Salad

Day 12
- **Breakfast:** Avocado and Poached Egg Sandwich
- **Lunch:** Lemon Garlic Turkey Meatballs with Green Beans
- **Dinner:** Blackened To-fu with Sesame Broccoli Slaw

Day 13
- **Breakfast:** Green Shakshuka
- **Lunch:** Chicken Casserole with Broccoli
- **Dinner:** Stuffed Bell Peppers with Quinoa

Day 14
- **Breakfast:** Baked Eggs in Avocado
- **Lunch:** Chicken Breast Stuffed with Spinach and Cheese with Boiled Vegetables
- **Dinner:** Cauliflower Steak with Tahini Dressing

28-Day Meal Plan

Day 15
- **Breakfast:** Coconut Flour Pancakes with Berries
- **Lunch:** Avocado and Turkey Wrap
- **Dinner:** Roasted Beet-root with Herbs

Day 16
- **Breakfast:** Sweet Pota-to and Spinach Breakfast Hash
- **Lunch:** Mediterranean Chickpea Salad
- **Dinner:** Butterfly Salmon Steak with Pes-to Sauce

Day 17
- **Breakfast:** Tropical Mango Coconut Smoothie
- **Lunch:** Zoodles with Pesto Sauce and Turkey
- **Dinner:** Mushroom Stroganoff with Creamy Garlic Cauliflower Rice

Day 18
- **Breakfast:** Chocolate Strawberry Smoothie
- **Lunch:** Quinoa and Black Bean Salad
- **Dinner:** Stuffed Zucchini Boats

Day 19
- **Breakfast:** Mint Chocolate Chip Smoothie
- **Lunch:** Shrimp Avocado Salad
- **Dinner:** Grilled Salmon with Avocado Salsa

Day 20
- **Breakfast:** Turmeric Ginger Detox Smoothie
- **Lunch:** Vegetable and Nut Stew
- **Dinner:** Baked Cod with Asparagus and Hollandaise Sauce

Day 21
- **Breakfast:** Peanut Butter Banana Smoothie
- **Lunch:** Tuna and White Bean Salad
- **Dinner:** Zucchini Noo-dles with Pesto and Shrimp

Day 22
- **Breakfast:** Quinoa Breakfast Bowl
- **Lunch:** Avocado and Turkey Wrap
- **Dinner:** Salmon and Asparagus Foil Packets

Day 23
- **Breakfast:** Greek Yogurt Bowl
- **Lunch:** Cheeseburger Lettuce Sliders
- **Dinner:** Spaghetti Squash with Fish Balls

Day 24
- **Breakfast:** Flaxseed Meal Pancakes with Berries
- **Lunch:** Chicken Casserole with Broccoli
- **Dinner:** Coconut Shrimp with Mango Salsa

Day 25
- **Breakfast:** Oatmeal with Fresh Berries
- **Lunch:** Red Lentil and Chicken Stew
- **Dinner:** Stuffed Bell Peppers with Quinoa

Day 26
- **Breakfast:** Spinach Omelette
- **Lunch:** Chicken Breast Stuffed with Spinach and Cheese with Boiled Vegetables
- **Dinner:** Cauliflower Steak with Tahini Dressing

Day 27
- **Breakfast:** Oat and Berry Acai Bowl
- **Lunch:** Mediterranean Chickpea Salad
- **Dinner:** Butterfly Salmon Steak with Pesto Sauce

Day 28
- **Breakfast:** Avocado and Poached Egg Sandwich
- **Lunch:** Mushroom Cream Soup
- **Dinner:** Greek Chicken Skewers with Cauliflower Rice

Conclusion

The "Galveston Diet Cookbook for Beginners" serves as more than just a collection of recipes; it is a comprehensive guide to achieving a healthier and more vibrant lifestyle. Rooted in scientific research, this cookbook introduces a transformative approach to eating that aligns with your body's natural rhythms, focusing on lasting well-being and sustainable weight management. The Galveston Diet, developed by Dr. Mary Claire Haver, offers a holistic lifestyle that goes beyond typical diet trends by emphasizing the importance of metabolic health, reducing inflammation, and supporting hormonal balance.

The Galveston Diet is based on the idea that food is a potent tool for healing and promoting your body's natural processes, not merely fuel. The diet combines principles of intermittent fasting with a focus on anti-inflammatory foods, which together create a unique approach to optimal health. Unlike restrictive diets that often lead to frustration and burnout, the Galveston Diet encourages you to enjoy your meals while making mindful choices that support your health goals. This balance allows for sustainable weight loss and improved metabolic health, which in turn leads to enhanced overall well-being.

The cookbook is designed to be a practical and inspiring resource for anyone looking to embrace this lifestyle. Whether you are new to the Galveston Diet or seeking to refresh your meal routine, this book provides the tools and guidance needed to succeed. It includes a 28-day meal plan that is carefully crafted to help you gradually incorporate the diet's principles into your daily life. The recipes are diverse, delicious, and designed to keep your meals exciting while aligning with your health objectives. From breakfast to dinner, and even snacks in between, each recipe is a step toward better health without sacrificing the joy of eating.

Embarking on the Galveston Diet is not just about following a set of rules; it's about making a lasting commitment to your health. The diet encourages patience and flexibility, recognizing that lasting change takes time. The emphasis is on long-term maintenance of little, steady changes rather than large, abrupt ones. This approach ensures that the positive results you achieve are not fleeting, but rather a permanent part of your lifestyle. As you experiment with the recipes and find what works best for you, you'll discover a new relationship with food—one that is nurturing, satisfying, and beneficial to your overall well-being.

The benefits of the Galveston Diet extend beyond weight loss. This diet promotes energy, lowers inflammation, and helps to regulate blood sugar levels by assisting your body's natural processes—factors that are crucial to maintaining good health. These benefits contribute to a more balanced and vibrant life, where you feel empowered to take charge of your well-being. The Galveston Diet Cookbook for Beginners is designed to be your companion on this journey, offering not just recipes, but also encouragement and inspiration to keep you motivated.

In conclusion, the "Galveston Diet Cookbook for Beginners" is more than just a recipe book; it is a gateway to a healthier and more fulfilling lifestyle. By embracing the principles of the Galveston Diet, you are committing to your overall health and well-being in the long run. This cookbook is here to guide you every step of the way with delicious and nutritious recipes that make healthy eating enjoyable and accessible. As you embark on this journey, may you find joy in every meal and success in your pursuit of a healthier, happier you. Happy cooking, and here's to your health!

Thank You

Thank you so much for purchasing this book and reading it all the way to the end!

If you enjoyed it, I'd be incredibly grateful if you could take a moment to leave a review on the platform. Your feedback is the best and easiest way to support independent writers like me and help me continue creating content that resonates with readers like you.

Your thoughts and feedback would really mean a lot to me and would help me keep writing the books you love.

Leave a review on amazon.com

Printed in Great Britain
by Amazon

49683071R00051